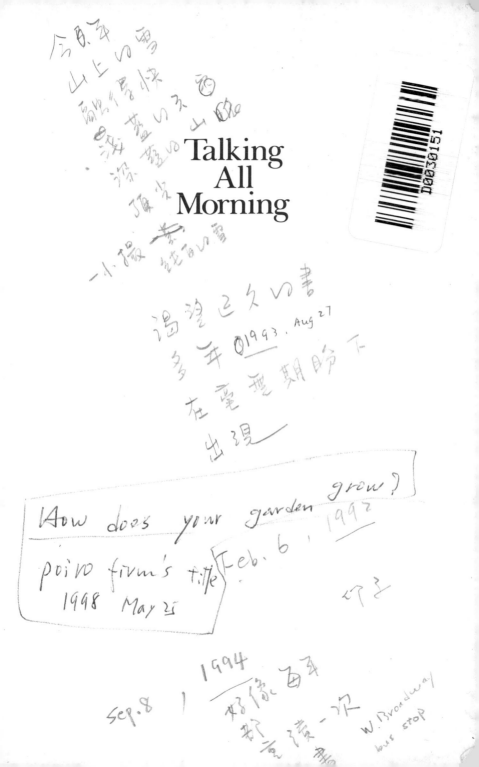

Talking All Morning

Poets on Poetry   Donald Hall, General Editor

Talking
All
Morning

ROBERT BLY

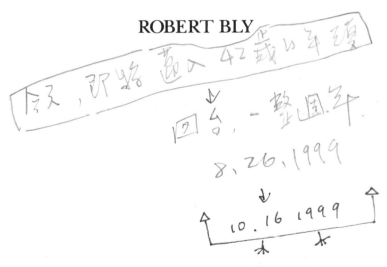

Ann Arbor   **The University of Michigan Press**

Bly, Robert.
Talking all morning.

(Poets on poetry)
1. Bly, Robert—Interviews.   2. Poetry.
I. Title.   II. Series.
PS3552.L9Z58   1980   811'.54   80-10789
ISBN 0-472-15760-4

Acknowledgments

Grateful acknowledgment is made to the following interviewers, publishers, and journals for permission to reprint adaptations, excerpts, and selections from copyrighted material:

The Ally Press for permission to reprint an interview with Robert Bly, "Poetry Is a Dream That Is Shared with Others," which first appeared in *Sucking-Stones.*

Beacon Press for permission to reprint "Leaping Up into Political Poetry" from *Forty Poems Touching on Recent American History.* Also for "Clouds Grow Heavy" from *The Kabir Book,* copyright © 1971, 1977 by Robert Bly, copyright © 1977 by The Seventies Press. Reprinted by permission of Beacon Press.

Boundary 2 for permission to reprint "The Aeroplane."

Brockport Writers Forum for material edited from a video-tape interview with Robert Bly in the Spring, 1970, sponsored by the Brockport Writers Forum, Department of English, State University College, Brockport, N.Y. 14420 © State University of New York.

Scott Chisholm for permission to reprint an interview with Robert Bly, "On Unfinished Poets."

Ekbert Faas for permission to reprint an interview with Robert Bly, "Infantilism and Adult Swiftness."

Kayak for permission to reprint "The First Ten Issues of *Kayak*," which first appeared in *Kayak*, no. 12, 1968.

Peter Martin for permission to reprint an interview with Robert Bly, "On 'Losing the Road'."

Minnesota Public Radio for permission to publish an interview by Bill Siemering with Robert Bly recorded in May, 1975, which first appeared in *Dacotah Territory*, no. 12, Winter-Spring, 1975-76.

Nation Associates for permission to reprint "Two Years After the War," by Robert Bly, May 21, 1977. Copyright 1977 The Nation Associates, which appears as "Post Vietnam."

New York Quarterly for permission to reprint an interview with Robert Bly and the poem "Looking Out to Sea" by Robert Bly.

Ohio Review for permission to reprint an interview by Wayne Dodd which first appeared in *Ohio Review* 19, no. 3, Fall, 1978. Reprinted with the permission of the editors.

Soho Weekly News, 111 Spring St., New York City, for permission to reprint an interview with Robert Bly, "On Writing Prose Poems," by Rochelle Ratner.

Street magazine for permission to reprint "A Conversation with Robert Bly," which first appeared in *Street* 2, no. 1, issue no. 5.

Texas Quarterly for permission to reprint "Conversation with Robert Bly," by Kevin Power, *Texas Quarterly*, 19, no. 3, Autumn, 1976.

Phil Yannella for permission to reprint an interview with Robert Bly, "Two Halves of Life," which first appeared in *Tempest* 1, no. 1.

Every effort has been made to trace the ownership of all copyrighted material in this book and to obtain permission for its use.

Contents

I

Inwardness and Biology

TWO LONG INTERVIEWS

The Evolutionary Part of the Mind

An Interview with Jay Bail and Geoffrey Cook

Inverness, California, April, 1971

What is so amazing in this century has been the blindness of the Americans. There is an incredible poetry in Spain, in South America, in Russia. Williams did not see it. Did Pound talk about . . . Pound almost never mentioned Rilke, for example. Why not? Because he's too inward for Pound.

You think that is really an attempt to go inside rather than . . . external.

Yes. I think it's a difference between the inner and the outer. And, as we know, Americans have always had this tremendous longing to stay in the outside life. Williams is a marvelous poet, and yet he insists that the surface of his poems shall be made up of objects. They'll hold closely to the exterior life. The novelists can't really write any more, because they're so interested in the externals of life. So I feel that . . . the opposite of that is when you go to someone like Lorca. When you go to Lorca you find yourself . . . you find yourself in the presence of a man interested in his own inward life. He's interested in his own desires, and he's interested in . . . he's interested in the interior life that's going on inside him. If you want to call that the interior animal life you can call it that. . . hummm? As opposed to the interior intellectual life. Then it turns out that this interior animal life cannot be expressed with images of . . . of curbs and broken bottles and the objects with which Williams hoped to express it. Can't be done. It can't be expressed with fragments from other cultures, as Pound hoped to express it. Can't be done. It can't be expressed with abstract words, as many of the Black mountain people hoped to express it. Can't be done. It cannot be expressed in English meter, etc. Absolutely hopeless. Can't be done. So the only way it can be done . . . it can only be expressed, I'm speaking now of what the Spanish believe, with what can be called animal images. That is to say, images that come from the animal . . . animal muscle blood part of the animal, and of the brain. And this is why Lorca is always going into the animal imagery. It's the fact that the interior animal life, the inward animal life, can only be expressed in images that are live and that pick up things from evolution and so on. This interior life goes way back into evolution and the only way to pick that up is to . . . Lorca isn't following these little stairsteps that the Americans try to make through the rational mind. He says things like this:

> To take the wrong road
> is to arrive at the snow.
> and to arrive at the snow
> is to get down on all fours for twenty centuries and eat the
>   grasses of the cemeteries.

> To take the wrong road
> is to arrive at woman,

woman who isn't afraid of light,
woman who murders two roosters in one second,
light which isn't afraid of roosters,
and roosters who don't know how to sing on top of the
    snow.

But if the snow truly takes the wrong road,
then it might meet the southern wind,
and since the air cares nothing for groans,
we will have to get down on all fours again and eat the
    grasses of the cemeteries.

I saw two mournful wheatheads made of wax
burying a countryside of volcanoes;
and I saw two insane little boys who wept as they
    leaned on a murderer's eyeballs. . . .

and since all roosters know is
    how to fly over the snow
we will have to get down on
    all fours and eat the
    grasses of the cemeteries forever.

Okay, let's see now. What can we compare this with?
Well, suppose we take a bad American poem, which
might go something like:

I left a school in Rhode Island
and I am walking on the knife edge of my awareness
and now I see around me the yellow desert
and your face is pale . . .
I have a new recipe for soup . . .

Here's Lorca again, a stanza of Lorca:

One day
the horses will live in the saloons
and the enraged ants

will throw themselves on the yellow skies that have taken
refuge in the eyes of cows.
. . . .
The living iguanas will come to bite the men who do not
dream,
and the man who rushes out with his spirit broken will
meet on the streetcorner
the unbelievable alligator quiet beneath the tender protest
of the stars.

So now the Americans, people like M. L. Rosenthal, for example, academic critics, will tend to say, "Well, that's a technique, you see, he's using a technique of imagery there." That isn't it at all. He's been able to, by using iguanas and alligators . . . he's been able to penetrate down into an evolutionary part of the mind.

In other words, you see this as going back to the sources, to the biological sources.

Right. Right.

Do you see this tradition springing up in North America? Who in North America do you see developing this tradition?

Gary Snyder is one who has understood and followed this—maybe John Haines. And Americans tried to go in that way a hundred years ago, with Thoreau, and with Whitman, and with Emerson. And again, they found that way through reading in the Eastern literature. Snyder followed that exactly. Very interesting. A hundred years later, the American writer again turns to the East, and again a certain part of his American mind is opened by this. And an entire generation now is moving in that direction. They are more interested in inwardness than either . . . than any of the academic poets were or any of the Black Mountain generation was. But talking about going back to biological sources, again Snyder has certain links there . . . because of what one is doing to some extent in meditation. After all, in meditation, you're sitting in the posture of the fetus and many of the people . . . a lot of people beginning in meditation often meditate on the breath. After all, breath is the one thing in our body that we have in common with the alligators and all the other creatures. It's the one thing we can't stop. You can't stop breathing. Therefore it has a deeper evolutionary link than any other thing in our body . . . . So anyway, always when you're involved in meditation there is a movement back into the past of the whole animal race. . . . This is very different, of course, from the Western idea of meditation, which is to go forward, farther, to get near the angels, get up into the light. . . . Whitman, you see, is interested in this biological link. He said, "I think I could turn and live with animals. They are so placid and self-contained. They don't sit up all night weeping about their sins. Not one of them makes me sick discussing his duty to God." Wonderful, wonderful. So, as far as the biological link, then Whitman had certain tendencies in that way too, but there are many other poets. . . . James Wright is very good in his links with animals, and of course Robinson Jeffers. A number of the younger poets, for example, Bill Knott, Pete Winslow. Also the surrealist work of Philip Lamantia. Surrealism has links . . . has this kind of link, not so much to the spiritual, but to the biological evolutionary part of the mind. So, again, the problem is that we've been cut off from that. And who cared about Philip Lamantia's work, all through the beat time era? Right? Nobody. Nobody cared about the surrealism. We've never cared for surrealism in this country. It's only the very younger poets who are doing it now with enthusiasm.

Let me shift a little. What do you think about the poet and politics? What do you think his responsibility is?

I don't think writing a poem exempts you from taking part in political work. The poet has a body also which in a certain sense is just the body of a man. . . . I remember when we first started doing poetry readings against the war, in 1966 and so on, in a sense we weren't even reading poems, just putting our bodies up on the stage. And it was clear from some of the people in the audience, if they'd had guns they would have been happy to shoot us. And . . . I've been . . . as it happens I took part in some things, I've been arrested for blocking an induction center and so forth. And when the police carry you off, it's interesting, they're carrying off your body, not your mind. It's just the body of a person.

What induction center?

The political . . . the induction center at Whitehall in New York. The same time . . . I think Spock was arrested on the same thing.

How did the cops treat you, etc?

It didn't amount to anything, but . . . where was I . . . is that . . . I mean, you write a poem with your mind, but you also have a body. And we could never . . . I remember, I could never get John Berryman up on one of those stages, and he always said, it's not my job to protest. My job is writing poetry. I don't know exactly what that meant—that if you write poetry you have permission to be schizophrenic.

Do most poets feel this way?

I think Charles Bukowski in Los Angeles would say the same thing. He would say, my job is to write poetry. It's not my job to protest. So, both the cooked poetry and the raw poetry in a certain sense in the United States is head poetry. Head poetry.

What kind of poetry, if any, is involved in actually putting your body on the line?

Well, that's not poetry. It's not poetry. It's just the act of a human being.

Would he tend to write different sorts of poetry than, say Bukowski wrote, or Berryman, just by the act that he felt that he had to put his body on the line?

Hmm . . . I think so. I think so. . . . It's interesting. In Russia, for example, where, from Mayakovsky on, it's always been understood that a poet has . . . has a kind of responsibility toward the society and toward political movement, which he can accept or not. That's understood there. And it's interesting that their poetry has a wider range than ours. Voznesensky has a wider range than any American poet his age. I'm just trying to give evidence for the kind of thing you said when you said, is it possible that poetry will be different, would be different, if the poet considered that he had a body, and that body could. . . .

Have you always felt this, since you were . . . say, twenty years old, that . . . that you ought to put your body on the line?

No. Not at all, not at all, not at all.

You personally.

Well, fifteen years ago the . . . there wasn't any line, you understand? No! There was a . . . kind of a general, an incredible loneliness with everyone alone in the room somewhere, very little sense of community.

But I'm still trying to stick onto you.

Right.

I want to know who you are.

And I . . . I had sense enough not to go to graduate school when I got out. So I went to New York and I lived there and, for a couple of years, by myself, and I must say it was first in solitude that I really felt an affection for the human community. Antonio Machado says that. But, then, I would confess, I was . . . I tried to take my experiences that I had in solitude and write poems touching on them, my first *Silence in the Snowy Fields* had virtually no political content of any kind. Matter of fact, when I began . . . then I wrote . . . after that, I . . . I'd always been . . . I became interested in the difference between Jefferson and Hamilton in the United States. And I became interested in the obvious sort of disintegration of the spirit that was evident in the fifties. And it must have had some kind of a reason. Then I wrote a book called *Poems for the Ascension of J. P. Morgan.* And these were . . . these were political poems mixed with advertisements, statements about political figures, etc., all mixed together. It was interesting. That was about 1958-59, no one would publish the book. That was before the times of political poetry. It was turned down by all the publishers I sent it to. And it simply . . . people simply didn't want political poems of any kind. Only Rexroth, Thomas McGrath, Ferlinghetti, were writing anything political. So, when I started to do work with the Vietnam war, others thought it was a surprise, though it wasn't a surprise to me.

Others thought it was what?

Others thought it surprising for a poet who seemed to be allied with the Chinese poets . . . with meditative poetry, to do this work. It didn't seem a surprise to me.

How do you reconcile Tibetan Buddhist beliefs with the war . . . with your antiwar activities?

I don't see any contradiction myself. I'm not sure that I have Tibetan Buddhist beliefs. I merely do some meditation.

You would not call yourself a Buddhist?

I don't think so. That's a pretty serious statement. I'm not sure . . . I think the ancient Chinese civilization that carried forward Buddhism is so superior to ours, and the conscious and the unconscious that they developed achieved such incredible spiritual adventures and power . . . as some of Charles Luk's books make clear . . . that we are truly barbarians. They're right. And I don't really know if the . . . if there's any American who has a conscious and an unconscious working together, a body and a soul working together so well, so beautifully, that he has the right to call himself a Buddhist. I myself doubt it. We're all just beginners. But of course one of the main Buddhist ideas is that the Westerners have got to stop . . . got to stop insisting on this distinction between the body and the mind and then choosing one.

Would you say that you were in your mind a lot?

Yeah. I am certainly.

Is one purpose of meditation for you to get more . . . ?

Yeah. Exactly. Get down out of the head and down into the body. That's also the purpose of chanting. And the same thing in American poetry. It's . . . it's . . . American poetry is trying to lower itself from the head poetry of the English and of the 1950s down into the throat and finally down into the gut. And it's . . . chanting merely . . . in other words, Ginsberg's poetry is still up in his head and in his throat. His chanting is in his gut. He's following his own voice down into his gut. Maybe he'll make it.

And what about Snyder's relation to this?

Well, Snyder has gone down as far into the body as he intends to go. In certain ways he's becoming more intellectual. And yet, it seems to me, he is the one American poet who has absorbed the main push of the Buddhist idea that your conscious and your unconscious should swirl together with perfect ease like layers of a lake or something. That all layers should all move together.

Does he actually put his body on the line? Politically?

. . . See, the word politically he would interpret differently. He would say that by removing himself up into the Sierras and making a place for himself there, he has taken a political action, his body's up there. In fact he has a new poem called "Front Lines," I think, which says, in fact, that the front line is up on the edge of the mountain now. Not in the city.

Don't you think also that those poets who say that a poet's job is just writing poetry and not putting the body on the line are saying the same thing?

It's possible. I don't know. I don't know if Snyder's right or not. But his position is thought out. It's not like Berryman's. It's not like Berryman's or the new critics who really despise their bodies and . . . and hate the body whether it's brought into politics or into meditation.

Do you still go into retreat occasionally?

Yes. Constantly.

Several times a year?

Sometimes five or six times a year. I also . . . when I'm living in Minnesota, we rarely see anyone. I see people when I'm out reading or doing something political. At home, we see no one. So I have hundreds of hours of solitude a month. I also have a shack; literally no one, not even my wife, knows where it is.

One thing I want to ask, and this is sort of . . . you do give benefits once in a while, don't you? Political, spiritual causes?

Yes. About a year and a half ago I gave a series of ten benefit readings in ten days around the country for the Resistance. Ed Sanders and myself and Creeley and

13

others, were traveling together. Wild! [Laughter.] Then, recently, I took part in a benefit for Chavez here, and a benefit for the Tibetans over in Berkeley. I believe in the benefit poetry reading. I believe in free poetry readings also.

Okay. Your experiences with meditation. First of all, could you tell me . . . tell me about your studies with meditation in relation to your work and . . .

Well, I . . . about . . . in the early fifties I spent a couple of years alone, about three years, some in the woods and some in a small room in New York. Part of that I did from an instinct, a desire to be alone, which is very powerful, and part of it because I was too poor . . . . Once I got alone, I was too poor to get out of it. So I was forced to remain alone, in a way longer than I'd intended to. But it turned out that that was . . . it was those years in which I learned everything that I tried to bring into poems.

This experience of aloneness is what a lot of young artists today are going through.

Right. The danger now, of course, is that . . . you see, it's interesting—when I was in New York at that time there was no . . . there wasn't any community. There were no communes, there was no one to go to. I would have loved to have gone to a commune so I could have eaten or talked to people but there weren't any around. And Ginsberg described that same kind of feeling, and he met Kerouac and a couple of others, but there were really very few. But the danger now is that there are too many communes, and too great . . . too much community. And so the poet goes off to a commune. Hell, he could just as well be in a university. Talks all day anyway. So solitude really is solitude, and it means no other human beings around, and merely being antisocial in a university is not sufficient. Snyder gained that solitude by going to Kyoto and of course doing a lot of meditation. Meditation is merely intensified solitude. So then I . . . then after a few years I came back and I got married and moved to a farm in Minnesota. By that time I'd decided not to ever go into the universities if I could avoid it. I began to do meditation on my own and then I went over to England to try to get some instruction in meditation. And I went to . . . by great luck I found, heard of a man, a Tibetan, named Trunpa Rinpoche who had opened a Tibetan monastery or study center in Scotland. So I went and studied with him . . . . That's a picture of him there. And he gave me instruction. So I continue to do meditation still and I . . . of course to me the Tibetan thing is very, very good. . . . One reason is that the Tibetans, in meditation and personality, are very much like the Spanish are as poets. They have deep biological links, they do a lot of physical things, physical work, they are not puritanical, they laugh a lot, they are not interested in authoritarian systems. So it's very interesting. . . . Zen training is built on an authoritarian situation, because the Japanese, the young Japanese, are so terrorized by the authoritarian system that the only way to break them of it is to reconstruct it and then work from there. The Tibetans evidently have not been terrorized in that way. It's hard to explain it but . . . despite what is called their feudal culture, which is now destroyed, it evidently was not an authoritarian culture. So, therefore, the relation between a Tibetan teacher and student is very free and easy, and full of laughter and jokes. . . . The Tibetans regard the Indians as all right except for their uncontrollable desire to speculate. Some long to live in the top of their heads. That's all right, they say, but body energy is good also.

about   Tibetans

The story goes that the reason why the Buddha came to be reincarnated in Tibet again and again in the form of the Dalai Lama is that the Tibetans were the most ferocious people on earth and they were the least meditative, so they really needed it.

That's right. That's right.

Supposedly a folk story. How does . . . ?

We need it pretty bad here, too.

Right now we do. We're coming, we're coming!

[Laughter.]

How does meditation affect you as a poet?

Hmmm. Well, it's possible it doesn't affect me at all. That's always a possibility. My poetry . . . will continue to be bad! That's always a possibility. The second possibility is that there's an inner space inside of you. And that in order to write poetry you must be in that inner space. It doesn't matter if you're limping along in it, as long as you're in it. Of course, Americans not only do not believe there's an inner space, they don't want to go in there anyway . . . they want to go to the moon. And the English want to be polite. They don't want to be in an inner space. So . . . but this is where the intense poetry comes from, like that of Juan Ramon Jimenez, a Spaniard, or Antonio Machado, in which they're inside the inner space, and then they're flying, too, an ecstatic quality of flying inside the inner space. Now what sitting, or meditation . . . I don't know, meditation is not a very good word, because it implies you're meditating on something; actually, what it really implies is sitting inside an interior space, do you follow me? That's why the Buddha often has a circle around him to indicate the boundaries of the interior space. And, in sitting, the hope is that you can go inside that interior space and forget this clumpy body that you've got hanging around your arms and legs. Then, what would happen is that the long experience of sitting would merely intensify the speed of flying and make you more at home in the inner space. So I think that to some extent . . . at least I feel more at home now in my inner spaces than I ever did when I was in high school or when I was five years out of high school. Poetry has had a part in that, but surely meditation. . . . So of course your question was phrased in such a way that you consider poetry more important than meditation. You didn't say to me: How did your poetry affect your meditation? That's interesting. It's probably the way an Oriental would have phrased it.

[At this point, several young kids come to the door of the cabin in which we are talking. Bly rushes across and engages in a minidiscussion which mostly centers around "What are you doing." Afterward, he comes back, satisfied, as though he had just finished giving a long, happy reading of his poetry.]

Ah, the red-haired one is mine. She's an Aquarius. How different children are, you know. I have another girl also, so different!

Let's move from . . . what is the relation . . . why did you make the decision never to go into the universities to teach?

Hmmm. For a couple of . . . well . . . you see, I'm in doubt as to whether to give you, you know, well-thought-out reasons or body reasons. But when I hear poetry be-

17

ing discussed in the classroom, I often get a nauseous feeling in my stomach. I don't know why that is, but I've felt it since I was in school. When I see an ecstatic poem . . . when I hear an ecstatic poem being described, being discussed in these calm, clear voices, nonpassionate voices in a classroom, I feel nausea. I didn't want to be nauseated the rest of my life so I decided not to do that. And another thing is, of course, the solitude—the link between poetry and solitude. And solitude is simply impossible in a university. You're paid to talk, not to be quiet. Also, the third thing, which has come on recently, is to watch what has happened to most of the poets—the poets of my generation who have gone into the universities. It hasn't been good. You're . . . several things . . . One thing that's happening is you're involved with the competitive power thing automatically in your department, and that's the exact opposite of what poetry tries to bring from us. So that's a disaster. Secondly, you're talking all the time. That's a disaster. Just the sheer physical act of talking can wipe out a great deal of poetry that's inside of you. The third thing is, you're talking all the time to people less mature than you, who have less experience. That's a disaster. And kids in the universities don't realize what a sacrifice grown-ups are making to talk to them all the time. Poetry can't be written in that circumstance. To write poetry constantly you need to grow . . . and in ancient times, for example, when the poet was not in the university, the chances are he was talking a lot to men and women who were twenty years older than he was, more mature than he was. But you put a poet in a university and he ends up talking mainly to students eighteen to twenty years old who know less than he does and are less mature. So, of course, what happens, if he's a good teacher, is that they worship him. That doesn't help either. That's another disaster.

So, I believe in good teaching if I were not a . . . if I didn't write poetry I might be a teacher, but I think it's suicide for a poet . . . for a writer. For example, I don't think that university teaching has been good for Creeley at all. At all . . .

How has it hurt Creeley?

Well, I simply see . . . I love Robert. And some of his poems I love tremendously. But I see his work becoming more intellectual. For example, there was a book called *For Love,* and then *Words,* and then *Pieces.* I think it's a . . . the sources of Robert Creeley's poetry are very obscure, that is to say, he's a very mysterious poet, and . . . so we can't say anything about that. But I do feel the effect of an increasing invasion of his poetry by the rational mind. And, since the rational mind is what you use when you're teaching . . . hmmm, mostly? . . . how can you ever hope to avoid it? Do you know Jung's idea of the four different faculties the human being has?

No.

Well, it's not terribly elaborate, but we could place intellect at the top of the circle, if you're an "intellectual." At the bottom, for an intellectual, then, would be feeling. And off at the sides are two others, one is grasp of facts, and the other is intuitive intelligence. Jung doesn't make a lot of this, he just says, well, those are four kinds of intelligence, and a human being tends to have one of them dominant. Now Frost is basically an intuitive poet. That meant that his intuition is at the top, his intellect is not too strong, his feelings are not too strong. His intuitive power is tremendous; his grasp of facts is very weak. So . . . . But what happens, Jung says, is that the danger is that . . . say, for an intellectual, let's say, like Robert Creeley or me or you . . . the intellect is the strongest. Now if you get into a profession in which you use your "dominant function," as he calls it, then there's a tendency for your weaker function to atrophy, to . . . right? You see that? So your feeling will get weaker. Jung was saying this, incidentally, to a whole group of psychiatrists in London about 1935, and he said, now all of you are intellectuals, and in feeling you are about thirteen years old. Your intellect is about fifty-five years old but . . . they were quite offended by this. And he said, this is all because you have developed your dominant function at the expense of your inferior. Okay. And then he said an interesting thing. He says, now, your inferior function, which none of you respect, is what links you to the whole human race. It's like a ground in a radio set. A great metaphor? Tremendous. So he says . . . now, he didn't make this remark, but surely we can extend it farther . . . namely, that poetry is written with the poet's inferior function. If you are an intellectual, your poetry is written with your feeling function. So Robert Creeley's first large collection is called *For Love*. That's right. It comes right down there on that feeling thing; he drives right down, throws this intellectual stuff aside and demands to talk about feelings. He's going to talk about feelings. He's not going to have lies about human relationships with women, he's going to talk about the feelings he actually has. That's what's so great about his work. But then we're talking about teaching in a university, and again, the feeling function is of no real significance in the university. You've got to repeat the idea stuff over and over and over and over again, you've got to convey ideas, always it's your superior intellectual function that's being called on, so naturally. . . . That's what happened to Robert Creeley, and I

don't know why I mentioned him, I admire his work a
lot, there are dozens of other poets, whom I don't re-
member now, but whose work, when I open their books,
I see is becoming weaker and weaker and weaker, from
one book to the next, and becoming more distant from
feeling.

Can poetry be taught more effectively? If it can, how?

I don't know. You see, I have not taught creative writ-
ing in a college, but if I were teaching creative writing, I
know what I would do. I would say to the people, any-
body who wanted to study poetry with me, I'd say, all
right . . . well, the class has how many creative writing
students? Fifteen? The university has to provide fifteen
little shacks somewhere out in the hills. And these stu-
dents go out there, and they have to stay at that shack.
If they're going to study with me three months, they
have to stay there three months. And I will visit them
once a week. They will show me their poems, we'll talk,
and that's it. And they're not going to see anyone during
those three months. Any tracks seen toward the shack,
they flunk. [Laughter.] Poetry cannot be taught well
without solitude. It's impossible. And that's why many
of the great poems that we know from China were writ-
ten after the man was fifty or sixty years old. Because
often what men did in China was to marry at nineteen,
and enter the civil service immediately, and have chil-
dren. After twenty years they were only thirty-nine. At
that point . . . their children are now grown-up, nearly
twenty years old. At that point they say goodbye to
their wife, goodbye to their children. They take to their
huts the Taoist books that they've been gathering, and
they go out to the hut for the last twenty or twenty-five
years of their life. And then they write their poetry. So

they have definite stages of life, and a man or woman passes through one stage and into another stage. But poetry is not really thought of at all in this country . . . it's thought of as something you can do at the age of twenty-one or twenty-two which I . . . I couldn't write a thing when I was twenty-one or twenty-two. My head was so full of gunk that it was impossible for a poem to come through it. Well, that's not much help in teaching poetry in the universities, but . . . that's what I would do.

I'd like to talk to you about Kenneth Rexroth, who is teaching creative writing at the University of Santa Barbara. He doesn't teach poetry. He has everybody in his class who wants to come in and bring songs. They have to write lyrics or whole songs. They come in and they perform the songs and sit around doing the songs and listening to rock music. That's one way of doing it, just . . .

Well, that's an alternative, he knows that the idea of having solitude for them during the time they're here is impractical. A university would not agree to that. So, what he's doing is trying to get them involved in their physical bodies through song, and get them out of their heads a little bit that way. It's a compromise. When a person is writing these song-poems, most of the time his or her intellect plays very little part in it. In solitude, your intellect takes part quite a lot, though it's subordinate. Anyway, I was very interested when I found out that Rexroth was doing this. I talked to him about it a couple of times. And I think he's having moderately good success. The problem is, that since most of the music they know is absolutely without solitude or any depth, they just repeat the junk that they hear. They're not really learning anything. They're just absorbing themselves in a finite layer of the American muck.

Yeah. Very Much. Okay. I'd like to get back to a subject which you . . .

I think Rexroth is a great man. I think he's really . . . he's the most fantastically . . . his poetry is greatly underrated. He's really a great nature poet. And also, the most intelligent literary man in the United States by like seven or eight times. And if we talk about evolutionary or biological poetry, Rexroth is the father of this kind of poetry in the United States. His images have . . . they have great resonance. Do you remember his image of the black and white cows lying down among the graves? Wonderful. Wonderful. The life style that Gary Snyder embodies in his poems, I saw first in the poems of Rexroth. And Gary's early poems really are mixtures of Rexroth's poems and the Chinese poets, just as my *Silence in the Snowy Fields* is a union of Rexroth and some twentieth century Spanish poets.

Yeah. I'd like to talk about the purpose of your press, which I believe is now known as The Seventies, *isn't it?*

Yeah.

Could you talk about what you feel about the press and the future of the press in relation to, let's say, the commercial press and the academic press.

Oh, yes, okay. I don't think my press is terribly important. I started the thing ten years ago because the poets I wanted to translate and publish, poets like Trakl and Neruda, would simply not be accepted by the big presses. Period. Never heard of 'em. So I put out the books. And how much influence it's had, I don't know. It's had some on American poets. Trakl is still not at all well known. Neruda is not accepted. The fools in the big publishing houses now will print Neruda. But there are younger poets coming along in South America who don't resemble Neruda and the big houses aren't going to print them. So therefore . . . you see, to me the poet is at home in the small press. I was really at home doing these books. I would translate them slowly; and the big press says, you want to do a selected poems, you got to have seventy-five poems, eighty poems. My God, you translate that, it'll take you three years and a half. So we would do twenty poems, which would take us long enough . . . I mean, we might spend twenty hours on a poem, so that's quite a . . . wow, that's fantastic work. But nevertheless we could control it ourselves, we didn't have to fight with publishers about the size of it . . . you bring the thing out, marvelous. Ten years ago James Wright and I did twenty poems of Trakl, printed a thousand of those clothbound, and I think it cost us $750. For which we maybe got back about $500. So for $250 you're able to bring a great poet into print.

I put out about eight books and all that it amounted to is that I drove a forties car during the fifties and a fifties car during the sixties. That's all it amounted to.

I've become very dissatisfied with the small press and the mimeo revolution because the people it was going to were the poet's friends, number one. Number two, a lot of them were given away and thrown away, and most of the rest went either to libraries or collectors.

Where do you want them to go?

To people that maybe aren't usually reached by poetry.

Why aren't they reached?

Because they have the feeling that somehow poetry is somewhere in the head.

Maybe they're right. Maybe they're right.

I mean, the effects of rock lyrics are reaching a great deal of people, are able to move. Poetry at one time was able to move whole nations, at least on a feeling level. But now in the modern technological . . . the American state, it isn't. Why not? What can we do . . . ?

You can't do anything. If you think about that too much you'll turn into a literary Napoleon. You understand me? The attempt to construct an empire. These people that are not reading poetry are not people for you to conquer. They are human beings and. . . . The great danger of looking at literature in that way, saying, why can't we get poetry out to all of the people, etc., is that in so doing, if you think that way, you would destroy the base of your own poetry. You mustn't ask anything back of your own poetry, least of all that it be read by five million. If you wish this, you will end up with the same kind of spiritual bankruptcy that Norman Mailer now has and is trying to live through. Novelists have been destroyed by that. Because it's possible for a novel to sell five million copies in the United States, the novel is dead. The novel has killed itself to get this. Poetry has always had. . . . If the poets were on television and were able to reach everyone, I'm convinced that poetry would disintegrate in a matter of five to ten years. Because the poets themselves would disintegrate. They would start thinking in these terms, not of what the poem has given them, not of the relationship they have to the poem, but of their relationship to the audience.

You are married to your poem, or you have a love affair with your poem, and what happens to you is the same as what happens to a movie actress, when her relationship is suddenly not with a man, but with . . . rrrrr . . . all those blobs . . . rrrr.

Did you feel this process starting in yourself at all when you received the NBA [National Book Award]?

You see, I think that the . . . yes . . . I think that the American writer is very . . . has a weak psyche in relationship to fame and to . . . much weaker than the European. The Europeans can stand a lot of fame, some resistance is built into them. With us, as everyone says . . . I mean, a novelist writes one good novel, one book of poems, he . . . rrrrr . . . he's gone. So when this thing, when the NBA was given to me, I thought it was a disaster. And I didn't want to accept it. But my wife said, "You've already refused two things; it would sound as if a habit had gotten started." So I decided to make a statement about the war with it.

I heard that you did something with the award itself?

Well, it was presented at Lincoln Center, and so I wrote a . . . you're allowed to speak for about five minutes . . . I wrote up a statement and then when I was given the prize was allowed to deliver this. The statement criticized the book publishing industry for not having made any stand against the war. [Laughter.] About halfway through, boos started to come up. It was very interesting. I had made arrangements with a young man in the RESIST office to receive the thousand dollar check. He started to come up the aisle . . . some thought it was a right-wing man with a gun. [Laugh.] That was a compromise, to try to use the money for something decent and to make a statement on the war at the same time. But I still go along with what Robinson Jeffers says. "If you have a poet, then listen to him but for God's sake, leave him alone. Don't give him prizes." This is what destroyed Faulkner and what made Hemingway play the fool. Wow! Tremendous poem!

At one time, I figured that if the government was very smart, the way it could get rid of most of the resistance in the United States . . . the vocal resistance . . . would be to give every artist and writer a grant outright, and then there'd be no more criticism.

They've done that, they've given a lot of grants. They started with a system of grants to publishers and writers, and almost all of the people in COSMEP [Committee of Small Editors and Publishers] accepted these grants. Ferlinghetti, you know, sent a telegram last year to the COSMEP Convention . . . he suggested that they take no more government money, the little magazines. I wasn't at the conference, but I heard about it. They considered it. I saw Lawrence later and Lawrence was very shocked the way the vote came out. His proposal that the little magazine editors accept no more money from the government during the war was defeated by something like sixty-three to thirty, two to one. And he said, I am amazed . . . little magazine editors are supposed to be standing for the independent and the outrageous against the commercial and the slick and, if you wave a little bit of money under their noses—dong!! Ferlinghetti was so disappointed that he resigned from COSMEP. I did too.

What do you think about government aid to art?

It's hard to know what to do. American writers have always hoped that the government would take some kind of interest in them. And when they finally do, it comes in the middle of the war. If you do believe in government help in the arts . . . I'm not sure I believe in it as a principle . . . but somehow we're going to have to postpone the acceptance of that until the war is over.

Maybe even further, much further.

Maybe even further. I think the health of American poetry has been strong precisely because it has no link with the official culture. Gary Snyder has talked about a subculture. I tell you it's very hard, say in a place like Sweden, to develop a lively poetry. You know why? Because the culture is hierarchical, and every poet is fed into a hierarchical system that goes right up to the government. And I can't quite express it; it destroys their morale in some curious way. In this country we have two streams of culture. We have a commercial culture, of Saul Bellow and the *Saturday Review* and all of that, and underneath there is another culture, not really touched by the upper stream; and we complain that we want to get up into there . . . But we should be . . . thank God we have it. Writers in Sweden now have a government salary.

It's all different. We have a different culture, a movement, the alternative society and the alternative culture . . . .

Yeah. But the thing that the subculture really has not developed is a sense of their own standards. It's true that the commercial culture is flabby and retrograde and totally out of touch . . . but it has some standards. The younger culture has to be not only spontaneous and politically alive, and noncommercial, but also to have standards. The problem with the mimeograph revolution is that its idea was to have no standards at all. And that was a disaster. To me. And the problem in the theater . . . to put on plays and let the actors do the whole thing. . . . It's all very democratic. But suppose that none of the actors in the play have any standards?

Okay. To answer that I think there are a couple of things happening. Now with magazines such as the Book Review, *critical interest is starting to even out the standards . . . or like* Nola Express *and* Kaleidoscope. *Trying to even out this. Rexroth states that the . . . how does he state it . . . that it's a democratic process but it evens out. And it's sort of like oil coming to the top. I think this is the way it's working. The only things that are asked for in any project is that everyone be creative.*

Well, it's too much to ask.

And the thing of it is that talent is coming together and that there are . . .

In poetry, it's very clear. A person who does not have someone to help him in poems, who does not have someone to tell him that this image is bad, and that's bad, and this is great over here, and this is the best of your lines, this is your worst of them has a hard time moving forward. . . . So what we're trying to do in setting up critical standards is not to set up a hierarchy . . . this poet is better than that poet, we're not trying to do that . . . but to help people to avoid wasting their time, so that they can move forward swiftly. Criticism is absolutely essential in these things. And it's very interesting to me, that in Russia . . . where the sense of brotherhood among the people of the subculture is probably even stronger than it is here . . . that the subculture has real standards which we don't have. The amount of criticism of Russian poetry that is printed is incredible. And, as you know, the underground papers in this country don't want to criticize poetry, they don't want to get standards. They just want to hug everybody. And Russia is full of . . . has more Eldridge Cleavers in it than it has Timothy Learys. There's a new magazine out called *Audience*; there an Australian poet discusses his visit to Russia—. . . traveling around two months in Russia with Yevtushenko. The day he arrives, two of his poems in Russian have appeared in a magazine with two million circulation. His taxi driver in Moscow recognizes him, talks to him about the poems. And out in the country, they're giving readings to several thousand students at technical institutes and engineering schools. [Laughter.] And these students not only want to hear Yevtushenko, they name other poets, younger poets, that they want.

I think this is what I'm talking about. About a broader base for the poets. Where in Russia poetry means something. Yevtushenko can put up a resistance to the government.

Yes, it's very interesting. The Australian poet was astounded. Everybody was interested in poetry. And Yevtushenko said, I don't know if the Russian Revolution worked, but I know that the cultural revolution worked.

There's a very touching anecdote at the end. A Russian writer on a visit to the United States, visited Detroit. He was a novelist. So after a while, he asked if he could speak to some workers. After considerable hemming and hawing, the American officials managed to get for him 350 General Motors workers in an auditorium. So the Russian comes on stage and talks . . . rrrrrr . . . after a while he asks: "What is your favorite American writer?" Total silence. [Laughter.] He doesn't get it. He says, "How about Hemingway?" Not one of them has ever heard of Hemingway. [Laughter.] The Russian novelist didn't tell it as an anti-American story, he just seemed so amazed, completely knocked out. It's depressing . . . what you sense is that the problem is really deep. It is really, really deep. Apparently, if you want to take a group and get them interested in culture, you can do it. The Russians have done it. The Russian workers are no more sensitive than our workers in Montana, I'll guarantee you. But the Russians control television. They didn't allow the slurp to come out of it. We've destroyed our whole culture with this slurp television. To go back to your earlier longing, it appears that as a writer, no matter how much you think about it, you're never going to get through to those 350 workers in Detroit. The only thing you can do is to work with your most serious art and create that, and then it will go to your friends, and gradually it will move out from there. If you want to help this process further, you destroy the television stations. That would be the only thing to do.

Yeah, those 250, those 350 workers in Detroit, they're along with the billboard culture. But I think in this country there are a hell of a lot of people who want to know what's going on in the cultural substrata, and want some path in.

That's right. That's true.

And I think there are more now than there have ever been . . .

It's true. Ever.

Why would you say that was now? Why now?

Russia never went so far into the father as we did. It's called Mother Russia. We don't have any writers like Dostoevsky. We have father-types like Sinclair Lewis. Do you think Sinclair Lewis could forgive a whore and live with her and so on as Raskolnikov did, and consider her a holy being, because she was a woman? Oh, boy. Sinclair Lewis is applying his father standards to women. They don't come up. So therefore . . . but recently we have more care for "mother earth." We're going to stop some pollution. It means we have more care for "mother nature." The link, then, that goes into culture really is a link through the mother, and what is precious in poetry is the inwardness and the love of animals. I think that's what's happening, and it's nothing trivial, it's a solid movement. It's a good moment for Western civilization and for the United States; but the question is, Sgyent-Gyorgi says, whether the father-types will destroy the earth before the consciousness is able to change sufficiently.

What do you think about Movement media as opposed to the establishment culture?

Well, I've noticed a disturbing thing that oftentimes . . . speaking of the establishment culture . . . the *Rolling Stone* will review exactly the same books in any given week as *Life* magazine does. [Laughter.]

I know.

They both reviewed Mailer's book this week. So, the Movement . . . people like the *Rolling Stone,* are much more open to the establishment than most people realize.

They've read *Life* magazine once too often themselves. One of the things that moves me about the younger people is the refusal to compete. I think that we're returning to the mother-consciousness ideals and therefore the competitiveness involved in science, which is essentially a man competing with the original substances on earth, will begin to slack off; probably scientific advances will slow also. And the competitiveness inside business will slow. But, with it all, the Movement isn't sure, really, yet, whether it wants to develop powerful mother consciousness, which requires discipline and concern, or whether it wants to take some quick shortcut, the American way.

Like acid?

Yeah. The problem with Leary is not that he wanted mother consciousness—he was a father-consciousness Harvard professor in the early fifties and dissatisfied with that. He could have gone to the Orient and said, I want to develop my mother consciousness. And they would have said, okay, sit down over there in a corner, and after ten years you will have developed some mother consciousness. . . . It can't be rushed, has to be done slowly. But Leary wasn't satisfied with that. He wanted to do things the quick way. And he guessed that acid was a very quick way to develop mother consciousness. Far too quick.

Doesn't really develop then . . .

Evidently not. Leary is related to the people who send over B-52 bombers to get it done quickly. Leary wants to develop mother consciousness by taking acid 252 times. But . . . he has not developed mother consciousness. What he has done evidently is to lose consciousness. He has lost both his mother consciousness and his father consciousness. He really has now no consciousness. Eldridge Cleaver, by contrast, began with strong mother consciousness, as many blacks do, and now has developed some father consciousness. . . . The blacks are moving toward father consciousness at the same time the whites are moving toward mother consciousness . . . . It's strange . . . Angela Davis has done something similar. And this is why Angela is so frightening to the whites. She developed it by studying Hegel with Marcuse. So both she and Cleaver are in certain ways whole consciousnesses. The contest between that moderate wholeness and Leary's lack of consciousness is frightening. The Movement is basically white: it wants to develop mother consciousness hastily, without physical labor, without meditation, without discipline, particularly without physical labor.

What is the Movement? Who are the people in the Movement?

I'm not a good one to try and answer that but . . . maybe I can express my own confusion. Because I've never really . . . myself . . . I've never really thought it through.

This is a good place.

Who are the people in the Movement? Is the Movement made up only of the ones who come up for trial, like the Berrigans, or, the Weathermen? How about people like Marcuse? How about all the people who are living in Volkswagen microbuses up and down the coast of California? My wife picked one up the other day . . . someone hitchhiking, and asked him what he was interested in, and he said, "Eternal bliss." So my wife said, "How do you go about it?" And he said, "I bought a word!" "What do you mean, you bought a word?" "I bought a word." It turned out there was a man living in San Francisco who was from India, or he looked like an Indian, and if you live with him . . . he talks to you for two weeks, then at the end of the two weeks he sells you a word for $49.50, which is your doorway to eternal bliss. And . . . so . . . she didn't ask him what the word was, because, after all, he had paid for it. [Laughter.] But he did volunteer the information that the first word he got didn't work. [Laughter.] And . . . that . . . there's sort of a warranty on the word, you can go back and get a second word later . . . [Laughter.] . . . This man is rejecting the standards, evidently, of the United States—or is he? Or is he really? After all, isn't that what happens to the man in Lincoln, Nebraska, who goes out at a Billy Graham rally?

Yeah, but he also works for a living for his home, family, country, and flag.

Hmmm. However, Marcuse also works for a living; so does Joan Baez.

But the guy in the micro VW bus maybe doesn't. And maybe . . .

But there's a couple of problems . . . why doesn't he work? To some extent it's because the economy doesn't want him. The economy does not need a lot of people, it only needs 30 percent or so of the college graduates. A kind of message has gone out from the head ant of the economy, saying to thousands and thousands of people in their twenties, we don't want you. Please stay away from the cities. Go off somewhere and scrape a living together from some vegetables. We don't want you and we don't need you, this is not a pioneer situation. And it has been able to *broadcast* this feeling of rejection: *"You are not wanted."*

But there's a glorification of this. Even though the guy in the VW bus understands the economy doesn't want him and doesn't need him, now there's a glorification of being outside.

Yes, but it's not entirely his choice. When Thoreau dropped out, it was his choice because everything said, "Come in, we need you, we need to build in Massachusetts, don't you leave." So his choice is not as clear as Thoreau's. In a certain sense he's being asked to drop out.

Yes. But in another sense which would be difficult for you and me to gauge, he might have made the self-willed choice to drop out.

Exactly.

Because he's nonverbal, it's almost impossible to tell whether he's done it himself or the government has pushed him out. So, under those circumstances, would he be considered part of the Movement?

I have noticed, that whenever a person begins to strip himself he or she becomes much more sensitive to plants, animals, and to certain kinds of religious experience. Maybe the Movement should be defined as people capable of being moved by plants.

In Cuba, to try to create a cultural revolution, they were

printing Sunday supplements to the papers and pub-
lishing Cuban writers . . . printing also translations of
Faulkner, and, what I'm trying to get at now, do you
really feel that if we're to create a saner culture, that there
is a need for a complete change, a complete reversal . . . ?

Pablo Armando Fernandez, a Cuban poet, was working
for *Lunes* [the Monday literary supplement of the main
newspaper] just after the revolution. . . . He told me
one time that in *Lunes* they decided to do a Picasso
issue. So they spent $120,000 on color plates of Picasso.
And Fidel got mad at him a little bit. . . . What are you
guys doing, $120,000! But does the Movement here do
that? No, they don't. They don't follow Cuba in this
respect. They tend to fill their issues with political stuff.
So when we have an opportunity to be flambouyant and
intense in culture, the upper stream doesn't do it, and
the lower stream doesn't do it either.

[At this point, the same children come to the door of the
shack again. Bly immediately breaks out into a rash of
smiles and falls into a short pattern of conversation
which is broken rather suddenly by a solemn admission
from one child that she doesn't know what "finished"
means. Bly tells her that the interview will be done
soon. This does not satisfy her. But she leaves anyway.]

I'll tell you another screwy thing. Talking about the cur-
rent change from the father-consciousness civilization to
a mother-consciousness civilization—don't you think it's
possible we may be going instead to a child-consciousness
civilization? Hmmm? . . . The child asks and hopes that
he will receive. And if he doesn't receive, he'll drop that
project and go on to another. Right. And Cleaver does
not ask. He wants something, he demands it. And Leary,
if you want to describe him as having gone into child

37

consciousness, you could do that. And that's why the conversation was so painful between Leary and Cleaver the other night. Cleaver humiliating him for one solid hour. It was like an adult talking to a regressed child.

They had an interview together?

Yes. Didn't you see it?

No, I didn't.

It was a one hour tape made by the two Angel brothers here in San Francisco. . . . The brothers went to Algiers . . . and it was played . . . the whole hour was played on the educational channel. And it's one of the most amazing conversations I've ever heard. One hour. In the course of it, Cleaver kept saying to Leary, we're sick of you middle-class whites and your advice to tune in, turn on, and drop out. That means acid for your children in the suburbs. To my people in the ghetto, it means dying of smack.

Algeria discovered that if you have a drug culture you will lose about 15 percent of your force as far as revolutionary work goes. And that's exactly the 15 percent that you need to crest over into a revolution. Leary had nothing to say to that. Cleaver kept demanding from Leary that Leary should tell people not to use acid. Leary has said in the past that the revolution would come about through taking acid. If he truly had consciousness, at this point he would have told Cleaver to go to hell, would have said, That's what I've always believed, and this is what I now believe. . . . Instead of that, he gave in to Cleaver, and at one point he said, "If anyone takes any kind of dope that postpones the revolution for ten minutes, that is a crime." And so Cleaver almost got him to say it. Leary went a long way. And the people I was with who like Leary a lot kept saying, "Come on, Leary, tell 'em, tell 'em, tell 'em." But Leary never did it. Doesn't have father consciousness, doesn't have mother consciousness. He has no consciousness. He just said, "Yes, massah, you right." Cleaver becomes the dominating white male, and Leary the compliant slave. Wow! It's the most fantastic meeting between two people that I've ever seen on television. For fifteen years the white . . . love . . . or dope revolution has been moving in a sort of female rhythm from the left, and from the right comes the black male angry stream . . . and suddenly these two substances move closer and explode in front of your eyes, and a man from each sits there and talks to the other, and it's kind of a blazing moment in American history. It sums up the last fifteen years in one hour.

What does it say about the next fifteen years?

I asked several people who had seen it what they thought and they said, "It means there aren't any gurus any more." They recognize that Leary was not . . . had been their guru and was their guru no longer. And the white ones cannot accept Cleaver as a leader. I think Cleaver is a leader . . . I think what we're coming into is a period in which leaders with father consciousness are going to be very important and . . . because the American . . . I can't say it . . . the American personality with its increasing mother emotions doesn't seem capable of going in one direction any more. Rock music is separating into fifty different directions, and they were unable to prevent Altamont. In fact, they even see it coming. A good Freudian or Jungian could have seen Altamont coming ten years ago. But what I see ahead is a very swift disintegration of all the structures of the society, the profession of plumbing disintegrating, the profession of electricians disintegrating, the profession of science disintegrating. . . . In fifteen years, every commune will have to have its own plumber and they'll give him free readings in the I Ching, you know, if he agrees to fix their faucets . . . . We'll have to do things ourselves . . .

Throughout this whole interview, with the exception of Angela Davis I didn't see one woman mentioned. And I saw a hell of a lot of men. What do you think about . . . are there any woman poets that you would . . .

You wonder why I didn't talk more about women poets. You didn't ask me about women poets.

Well, no, but I didn't ask almost anything about any poets.

We were mainly talking about the stream of ideas in this country, which has been created and dominated primarily by men. That's why we end up talking about men when we talk about ideas. And this is one of the complaints that women have about the mainstream of ideas, is that it has been dominated by men. Erich Neumann in his book *The Origins and History of Consciousness* says that for many hundreds of years, during the matriarchies, men were trapped inside what's called the circle of the great mother. They could not get out. Eventually they did, and then with Hercules, Socrates, and Descartes instigated a still-flowing stream of thought, in which the main interest lies in masculine growth, in the political and psychic growth of a man. The man in this stream of thought escapes from the mother, then develops masculine consciousness and perhaps at a later stage of the story reunites his yang consciousness with his yin consciousness. This is the myth about the boy who leaves the village, goes to the big father city, develops into a man, and maybe becomes a human being at the end, maybe not. It's only recently that women are once more returning to thought about their own spiritual journey, and they look around and the men's literature does not help them. So many of the women I know are . . . know that they are. . . . They read Anais Nin, particularly the third volume of her diary, just out, Doris Lessing, also some of Neumann's work, especially *Amor and Psyche.* But Neumann says, I do not understand the psychology of the growth of women. A woman has to write these thing. Esther Harding *has,* since that time, and Marie Louise von Franz. Denise Levertov is a marvelous poet and deeply involved also in the biological poetry that we were talking about earlier. She is extremely important to many younger women that I know.

You have a theory about the three different minds of man. It sounds very much like some spiritual things that are around, particularly like theosophy.

This whole subject is another immense thing like mother consciousness, and I'm not sure how much time you want to spend on it. But this isn't theosophy. We're talking about the research of one of the best neurologists in the United States, Paul MacLean; he publishes primarily in medical journals. However, his work is summed up by Arthur Koestler in his last book, *The Ghost in the Machine.* And the gist of it is this: human beings all believe that they have one brain and that it can unify their life. This is the primary error. In evolution, when we changed from a fish to a mammal we changed the body, altered it, but in the brain, that did not happen. What happened was addition. The reptile brain is absolutely in-

brain

tact, at the base of the skull. It's been known a long time as the limbic node. Then when we became a mammal, the huge mammal brain was folded around the reptile brain. That's also been known for a long time as the cortex. Now these two brains have separate nervous organizations. They have separate functions. In late mammal times, the third brain was added. No one knows why. It's immensely complicated. About an eighth of an inch laid around the whole mammal brain. It's been known to the geographers of the human brain for a long time. It's called the neocortex. However, what MacLean has illustrated is that these three brains have their own systems, and there is no central organization in the brain. And this has very scary implications for the whole conduct of life. For example, a man can be dominated by one of his three brains. Actually, during the day, you are not living in any one of the brains permanently. You may live in it for two to three seconds and then flip to the next brain. And then to the next brain. You have done this since you were in the womb, and don't recognize the movements; the transitions are smooth. But if someone hits you, or threatens your life, you jump abruptly into the reptile brain, which is the preservation brain. You'll notice a completely different mental atmosphere. It may be certain kinds of fears, and sweat on the body; it may take ten minutes in those cases before you return to your mammal brain. Some people apparently get trapped in one of the brains: a cold war militarist may be trapped in the reptile brain. It's no accident the peace was called the cold war because the hostility is basically an act of the reptile brain. Men evidently have a tendency to stumble into the reptile brain; women have a greater channel into the mammal brain. The third brain is called the new brain and in it is some of the spiritual energy of man. When you see the pictures of Buddha with the light around his head it evidently means that Buddha has moved almost entirely into the new brain, out of the other two brains. When that happens, as in the Transfiguration, the whole body gives off light. There are stories of old Tibetan meditators who sit in a room reading a book by the light of their own bodies. We have never understood this well.

Do you believe that one of the best ways to move into this mammal brain is through meditation?

Perhaps every time you make love you move more deeply into the mammal brain and away from the reptile brain. That's what the statement make love not war means. I suspect that meditation is a way to transfer energy from the reptile brain to the mammal brain, then from the mammal brain to the new brain. That energy can be transferred, that is the hope of . . . that is the point of meditation, of everything. And Christianity suffered a severe loss when it lost meditation.

But meditation much more than say chanting?

Chanting is mammal, I think. Chanting takes you out of the rational part of the being and into the mammal. Maybe farther, I'm not sure.

The recent generation and my own generation to some extent have been moving away from the reptile to the mammal brain. Poetry has gotten warmer, more mammallike, and the sense of community has increased. The only problem is that the recent generation does not read enough and does not study enough. The new brain is fed by spiritual ideas. For a long time, spirituality has been condemned and despised by the older generation and study is despised by this generation so that energy has been draining away from the new brain and into the reptile . . . rock music is mammal music. It doesn't help you to get into the new brain, it probably drains energy from the new brain.

What about acid?

You can think of it as . . . acid as a way to penetrate into the new brain without any preparation. But the acid freak falls right back into the mammal brain. The new brain cannot be entered safely without great care. In China a thousand years ago, apparently hundreds of Taoists and Buddhist meditators were living in the new brain. They said we affect a revolution in China through the new brain. We radiate out from the new brain the serenity and affection which eventually changes the political system. The new brain was called White Clouds, by the way.

I'm working on a new issue of my magazine, to be devoted to the relationship between poetry and the three brains. Lorca sometimes takes an image from the memory banks of the new brain. He is constructing a model of the human brain in the guise of a surrealist poem.

Okay, let's move away from that now. What sort of symbol do you think you represent to the people who listen to you reading poetry? Particularly the younger college kids? How do you think you appear to them?

Well, I don't know, and I'm not very interested. If you ask a poet what sort of symbol are you, he has to think about himself as if he were a third person. He has to become an object. So I dislike talking about myself, in that respect. But there is one . . . poetry readings have been important for the growth of American poetry. The voice is actually more sensitive than our intelligence to certain truths, and it has more of a sense of community. It comes from the mammal brain. It comes from the stomach. I think one reason for the increasing range in American poetry in the last six or seven years has been the poetry readings. The danger of them is that when you're reading a poem, two things are being communicated—your personality and the poetry. And the problem, actually, is to try to help the people listening to respond to the poetry, not to your personality. It's easy to send out "personality." Then they're not . . . then everything is lost. Including yourself.

Do you see yourself as part of a movement toward a new consciousness?

I hope so. I hope so.

Yeah, and this is, I imagine, for the same reason that you talk very little about yourself throughout the interview.

Well, you haven't asked me any questions directly about my life, but I really am tired of interviews in which the poet talks about how he writes, and what other poets think of him, and all of that stuff. I prefer to talk about ideas. We all share ideas. Also, one of the reasons I don't talk about myself very much is that I'm a Capricorn. Capricorns love to hide things. And I'm a middle-western Lutheran. Middle-western Lutherans love to hide things. In fact, my whole generation grew up writing "hiding poetry" . . . that is, poetry that hides the major facts about yourself. I am working on a new long poem, which I've been working on since 1965, in which I try to overcome that somewhat. I do feel that in the nation many things are coming up from underneath. In a poem I say:

I am only half-risen,
I see how carefully I have covered my tracks as I wrote,
how well I brushed over the past with my tail.

So . . . Ginsberg was a great man in leading this openness and willingness to talk about yourself directly. That's the great gift he gave and for which everyone loves him. Robert Creeley also. As a Capricorn I learned very late. Capricorns do.

I remember that you said to me . . . that you said once, you really dig reading a poet's work, but every once in a while you like to flip through the biography to see who's there, who's really there. And I think that was the reason behind my question. I'm interested to know who's there, who's really there besides the ideas. And I think we touch on nothing like that throughout the interview. But that's okay. I imagine it's what has to be.

Well, this interview is long enough already. But . . . to some extent what you put in an interview is what you do not put in a poem. And what I'm trying to put in poems now is my own life.

Going Out on the Plain in the Moonlight

*An Interview with Cynthia Lofsness and
Kathy Otto, with Fred Manfred*

Madison, Minnesota, Spring, 1966

Would you like to tell us something about your back-ground?

Well, let's see, what story should I tell this time? I was born here in Madison, on a farm. I went to high school here and then enlisted in the Navy. It was in the Navy that I met the first person I had ever met who wrote . . . a wonderful guy named Izy Eisenstein from Portland, Connecticut. Izy wrote the first poem that I had ever seen a living human being write . . . I was dazzled . . . astounded. I still remember the poem. It was a description of the south side of Chicago, and it said, "The slums of Chicago are like a running sore on the body of Chicago." I thought . . . this is beautiful . . . how could he ever think up something like that all by himself? It was creation! At that time I was reading Somerset Maugham's *The Razor's Edge,* and I thought that was pretty far out. When I got out of the Navy I went to St. Olaf for a year and then transferred to Harvard where I graduated in 1950. At Harvard I knew lots of people who were writing . . . John Ashbery, Frank O'Hara, Kenneth Koch, and Donald Hall were all there, and

Archibald MacLeish was teaching there . . . students who have later become more or less notorious. There was a wonderful air of seriousness about poetry; many people at Harvard had intended to become poets since they were twelve or thirteen years old . . . this is something one rarely met out in the Middle West.

When did you first realize that you wanted to become a poet?

At St. Olaf I started to write poems, and then when I went to Harvard I decided to be . . . well, to go ahead; to be a poet is different from writing poems. Then I lived by myself for about three years rather than going to graduate school. I lived in Northern Minnesota for a while and then I lived alone in New York for a couple of years more. . . . I got nowhere, but I was able to do a lot of reading and thinking that the poets who had stayed on in school were not able to do.

When and why did you begin publishing The Fifties-Sixties *magazine?*

I was married in 1955. The next year I received a Fulbright grant to go to Norway to translate some Norwegian poetry into English. In Norway I found the work of many poets in the Oslo library . . . men like Pablo Neruda, Juan Ramon Jimenez, Cesar Vallejo, Georg Trakl, whom I had not known.

They were available in the Oslo library, but I had not met them in America. It became apparent to me how isolationist America was in relation to European and South American poets. These poets were well known in Europe, even in little countries, but totally ignored or unheard of in the United States. It became apparent that a good service could be done and that would be to start a magazine publishing some of these poets in translation. I felt avenues opening into kinds of imagination that I sort of dimly sensed somewhere off on the horizon, but I had never actually seen in English . . . Oh, I had seen half a line, or five lines dealing with this (imagery), but in the poets I've mentioned you find this imagery for twenty and fifty and eighty lines long. . . . Wonderful imagery, exuberance, and enthusiasm. If it interested me that much, it would, must, interest some other young poets. I imagined the magazine to be, not for the readers, but for the poets; I put it out for poets basically and therefore we didn't care about the circulation and we published as high quality criticism as we could get. We didn't give a damn if the readers liked the magazine or not . . . the usual magazine criticism is written to be a bridge between the poet and the reader. It tries to say some nice things about the poet and so entice the reader. It tries not to be too serious, and so scare the reader off; but I think this whole idea of criticism is bankrupt. We ignored the general reader completely and talked directly to the poet. We embarked on the criticism of younger poets . . . at that time the poets such as Creeley and Simpson were only thirty and thirty-two years old, but we published an essay on them as if they were seventy or eighty years old and tried to discuss what they had done so far in their work and tried to make criticisms that would be of real value to the poet himself. These two aims still are the basic idea of *The Sixties* . . . namely, to publish European poets in good translation that are ignored in the United States; and secondly, to give the poets some sort of criticism other than . . . he is very good, or he is no good at all. When my wife and I came back from Europe in 1958 we settled in an old farm-house. With William Duffy as the other editor, we put out our first issue.

What languages do you speak and how did you learn them?

I took some German in school, and some Greek. Later I applied for a Fulbright to Norway to translate Norwegian poetry into English. The Fulbright Commission gave me the fellowship even though I knew no Norwegian. They arranged for me to learn Norwegian while I was there . . . we went three months early and so by November I could read newspapers and by January or February I could translate and was able to finish my project. Swedish and Danish were easy after Norwegian, and then I taught myself Spanish in order to read Neruda in the original . . . and then some Italian. This is all I know. Except for the Scandinavian languages, which I know well, and Spanish, which I know fairly well, in the other languages my knowledge is sufficient to make sure that the translations I receive are accurate. I had to know something about these languages in order to check the translations that come in.

As both a poet and translator, would you discuss the difficulties you face in trying to restore the beauty of one language into another?

There are several kinds of translation. . . . There is the sort in which the man or woman goes flat-footedly through the poem and literally translates it word by word. That can kill the poem, and that is what has happened in the United States—the translations have been done for the most part by professors and semantic experts who know nothing about the English language.

Then there is another method of translation in which the person rewrites and revises the whole poem . . . a man like Ben Belitt at Bennington does that kind of translation, and it is hideous. Robert Lowell also did that in his book called *Imitations*; he defended himself by calling it that. It is not a translation. In the third kind, you try to be as accurate as you can and yet catch by care in language the *emotional tone* of the original man. It becomes a matter of how well you can use words and rhythm in English . . . so that whatever tone you are using depends on the emotion that you are trying to make blossom in the poem. What you are essentially doing is slipping for a moment into the mood of the other poet . . . into an emotion which you may possibly have experienced at some time. If you are able to remember or feel that kind of emotion, then you could translate that poem. Some poets have an emotional range that will be beyond yours, and if this is the case, you may just as well give it up, because you will just ruin the poems of that poet.

Would you draw some comparison between the creativity involved in writing your own poetry and that involved with translation?

When you are writing a poem, it is like going out on the plain in the moonlight, naked. You can dance around anywhere . . . you can run eighty feet this direction, eighty feet another, and so forth. Doing a translation is like going down the road in the moonlight, but you can only dance two feet on either side of the center . . . while still having to give the same feeling of joy as if you were running madly all over the landscape.

Haven't you and James Wright done some translations together?

Yes, we've done a lot of them.

Isn't it twice as difficult for two poets to achieve the same emotional tone of the original poet? ... or using your expression, to dance down the same narrow road without bumping into each other?

Well, we don't always work on the same poem. He has an incredible gift for language and is surely the best translator of poetry in the United States. What happens most often is that one of us will find a poem, work on it, plunge into it, and then the other one will try to pick up errors. Occasionally we will tackle poems together. The matter of tone is so important . . . to catch exactly the right tone. In most translations, one of us did the major work, the other the minor touching up. In the case of the Trakl book, we just decided it wasn't worth trying to distinguish who had done the work on any individual poem. I would think it might be difficult to adopt a tone for a poem if two people were working on it together from the start . . . it almost seems impossible.

What is your opinion of poetry workshops? Do you think they are successful?

In America there is an obsession with technique. . . . We are determined to win our wars by using superior technique. We have got wonderful, magnificent boots that have steel plates in the bottom so pongo sticks can't come through and they cost $80 a pair . . . and there are helicopters. The Romans had to make do with crosses, you know, but we have better things . . . helicopters, napalm, but it's all the same business. Instead of trying to think, to imagine what the people want, we are going to use technique and defeat them no matter what they think. We have to abandon such stupidity. The same thing applies to poetry. . . . If one wants to write well. My advice to anyone if he wants to write is to go and live by himself for two years and not talk to anyone. At the end of that time he would have some experiences that were different from the experiences that the other members of his family have had. And it is these experiences that he can use in his writing. In other words, to write well, the poet should have experiences of deep solitude. Instead of that, we send them to workshops where they live exactly like other people do and have exactly the same lack of original experience. They have no original experience; all you give them there is technique . . . it's that same fatal American mistake all over again, emphasis on technique and not experience, humanity, and personality . . . the whole workshop idea is really self-defeating. If we were in another country where emphasis was placed madly upon experience, it might be valuable to emphasize technique, but in America where every fool emphasizes technique, a workshop simply increases the coldness the man has been subject to since he was a boy.

Your comment that the poet should go off and live alone for two years and not talk to anyone . . . did you mean that literally?

Absolutely!

And the part about not speaking with anyone?

Yes . . . you know, I have had people come up to me and say, "I want to be a writer; what should I do?" I tell them to go off and live for two years alone, and then I can see in their eyes a look of, "Well, I don't want to be a writer that badly." They want you to say, "Go to the University of Washington . . . go to the Writers' Workshop at Iowa" . . . but such trips amount to nothing. In other words, you cannot be a writer unless you are willing to sacrifice something. To go off and live by yourself for two years is sacrificing very little. If you can't sacrifice that, you are not seriously interested in writing. It is not a matter of testing people, either. You have to find out who you are before you can even write one word that is of any value; and we have got it arranged so wonderfully in America that no one will ever find out who they are if they live their life the way everybody lives it. That is why we have it arranged, and that is the point of the whole thing . . . to prevent anyone from finding out who they are, and it works magnificently.

Since this person is going to be absolutely all alone, would it make any difference what environment he chose . . . perhaps another country?

No, I suppose it doesn't matter. It's been interesting that the people of fifty years ago who went off into solitude often went to Europe for that solitude. It has become clear in the last few years that "American earth" and a certain fresh solitude are no longer considered incompatible.

Fred Manfred: Can you give something definite . . . an example?

In the 1900s America was considered to be vulgar, and corrupt; those who felt that "corruption was not compulsory" . . . they meant intellectual corruption to a certain extent . . . Europe called them away. Pound went to Europe, Eliot went to Europe, Cummings went,

Cummings came back, Hemingway came half-way back; Eliot and Pound never came back. But they got away and found something valuable. What has been happening lately is that people feel that if there is going to be a fight, it should be fought out here; Eliot, after all, gave up his American citizenship. I don't know any American poet or writer now that would seriously consider such a thing, anymore than you can imagine Yevtushenko giving up his Russian citizenship. So there is some common sense and health in the last thirty years in relation to America, in that the poets do not feel superior to it, but they feel they will fight it here on this ground.

When you look at other literatures, it becomes obvious that unless a poetry can come directly out of the ground of the country, it will never last. In the case of Pound and Eliot, we see literature which is grown in flower pots. Take those flower pots, magnificent and flowery as they are, across the ocean and put them in New York or anywhere in America; they won't take root and grow because they weren't created in this country. This is one reason that the modern revolution in the 1910s died out in the 1930s. What has happened is that writers now have started all over again . . . men like William Stafford, who was born in Kansas. I never expected a poet to come out of Kansas. Evidently that place is really barren, but Stafford came out of it and has written magnificent poems about Kansas. Then he taught in Indiana and is now in Portland. He was a slow starter; he published his first book when he was forty-eight . . . that was a book called *Traveling through the Dark* which won the National Book Award.

And Tom McGrath is living in North Dakota. He started writing poems when he was on threshing rigs up in North Dakota, and he has moved back here recently. James Wright is from a steel mill town in Ohio. Had he been born forty years ago, with his hatred of the way the industrial landscape has destroyed everything he knew as a child, he would have been in Europe permanently. Instead of that, he has written about Ohio and has lived in the Midwest for years. The tone of his poems expresses the fact his willingness to struggle with the United States, and in fact he is convinced that the United States, no matter how anti-literary, anti-intellectual, or vulgar, will never break his back. The title of one of his books is *The Branch Will Not Break*. I suppose my own book, *Silence in the Snowy Fields*, has something to do with my conviction that unless American poetry can grow naturally out of American ground, we may as well give up now and quit. I haven't written poems about Minnesota because I think it is the most poetic place in the world, but because if poetry is any good, it can live anywhere; it must be able to live anywhere, Minnesota is not worse or better than any other place.

You were surprised that a poet like William Stafford could come out of a barren place like Kansas, and yet, wouldn't this be the ideal place for the necessary isolation and solitude you spoke of earlier?

Several considerations are involved. One is a certain level of literary culture. Before solitude can give any nourishment to the poet, evidently a certain level of literary culture has to be reached. For example, in New England in the mid-nineteenth century, let's say the level of literary culture was five feet deep on top of the ground. The sensitivity went out to the Appalachian mountains and stopped there, being only say six inches deep in the West. It is interesting that in Melville's high school class half of the people went West and half went East. Now if Melville had gone West, the chances are that he would never have written anything. Instead he went East, that is to say he went to sea, and thereby remained within the magnetic area of that high literary culture of New England. Bret Harte is an example of the men who went West and found solitude out there, and yet, there is that quality of mystery missing in their work ... and it's not good work. When we come now to the twentieth century, the level of literary culture has reached out to about the Mississippi River. The culture is not as high as it was in New England, but has some depth. Almost all of the great writers that we know of in the older generation ... the Hemingway generation ... were born within fifty miles or so of the Mississippi River ... Faulkner, Hemingway, T. S. Eliot. The writers that were born farther West still didn't find what they needed in their youth. We don't know any poets from Idaho, except Pound, and we don't know any poets from Montana. Robinson Jeffers is a man from New England. ... He had a tremendous depth of literary culture under him ... and then he went West, way out there in Carmel, but he was a man of determined and tremendous strength, and he set up his tower out there and he carried everything in New England with him. In another twenty years the invisible wall at the Mississippi ... I mean we're using this weird metaphor as if there really were walls ... will probably break and some sensitivity will flow over the whole country. Then we may have a great poet from Arizona. That is why I said Kansas seemed to me to be beyond the bounds. That a poet as great, a poet with an imagination as resilient as Stafford's, could come out of there really bodes very well for the literary future of the United States.

In one of your articles you stated that the European influence on modern American poetry had become al-

*most nonexistent, though at one time it had been fairly
strong. How do you account for this decline in European
influence?*

One obvious cause was the depression, which pulled
everybody in America into themselves, and also pre-
vented them from getting away physically. The genera-
tion just before that, the Hemingway generation, came
out of the twenties which was a very affluent time. They
made use of favorable exchange rates, and could live in
France on $20 a month. When the depression came, all
that extra flow of money shut off, and fewer people
went abroad. Secondly, the depression made them real-
ize America was a suffering country, and they stayed
home and tried to help it. For that reason they were
somewhat shut off from the European influence. The
Second World War, as wars do, exhausted the nation for
about fifteen years afterward. In 1945 the people got
home, but criticism never did recover . . . it is just a sheer
matter of psychic exhaustion after a major war like that.
By the fifties America's living standard had become so
high, and America had become so arrogant, that it was
assumed that since we had such a high living standard,
we also must have the highest literary standards . . . "The
South Americans can't even feed and clothe themselves,
how could they write anything worth while?" . . . Why
bother to look abroad?

Another important factor was the isolationist New
Criticism of Cleanth Brooks, Tate, and John Crowe
Ransom in the thirties and forties. They broke abruptly
with Eliot's and Pound's fertile internationalism which
looked to the French and to other foreign poets. In-
stead, Tate and Ransom pulled in their horns and told
poets to look to English literature . . . so typical of
American universities. . . . But since these New Critics

really took entire control of English departments, they taught their students that everything they will ever need will be found in John Donne. It is much like a mother who tells her children to use stones for soup . . . everything they need to live on is in the stone . . . just put it in the water and boil it . . . it is very tasty, they say . . . and nourishing. The children just starve to death. Poets in 1950 were suffering starvation from lack of European influence in literature. Since then, the situation has begun to change, but still the arrogance of America remains, as the Vietnam war makes obvious. Johnson's trouble was that he confused the South Vietnamese people with Mexicans . . . he figured he knew how to handle Mexicans being a Texan . . . you push them around for awhile and they will give in. The important thing to see is that everything that happens in literature happens to the whole country. Everything that happens to the country happens to the literature. America will have to make a terrific effort to escape from its arrogance in foreign policy and its stupid feeling of superiority to the Asians. You can also see what agonizing labor is required for poetry to free itself from these feelings . . . the poets see the issue more clearly, at the moment, than the politicians.

Would you please comment about this country's image of the poet and the poet's image of himself; in an article of yours in The Sixties, *you mentioned that almost all countries . . . especially Ireland, France, and certain South American countries . . . had a clear image of what a poet is. The only exception to this was the United States, and I believe you said that there is no clear image of the poet in America today. How did this come about? . . . Why would it come about?*

Well, that is a good question . . . and the question can

also be put in this way. Why is it that in Russia there will be ten thousand people at a poetry reading, and what's more, moved — . . . half the women in the audience will be crying and some of the men too. It's the same question. There are several possible answers. One is that we do not have a people who have lived on their land for a thousand years as the Russians have. Instead we have people that have come only 100 to 150 years ago from many different European countries. Those countries had strong literary standards and a powerful literary culture. But immigrants are ashamed of their country in the first generation. The parents refuse to teach their children Norwegian, . . . they consider that old stuff . . . "Stop jabbering in that old language." . . . and the result is that these Americans forget, with an overpowering psychic amnesia peculiar to immigrants, the literature of their own country. So the literature is literally driven out of the psyche, since the only literature they know is in a language they have driven out of themselves. They try to become American . . . and here they are, trying to learn English. Therefore, it is not surprising that we have no image of what a poet is, for in order to have that, you have to have seen poets living on your own ground, where you live. Do you think I am making any sense, Fred?

FM: Yes . . . and the same thing is true of the novelist . . . Faulkner is really the first American novelist in the sense of America, even more than Hawthorne or any of the other ones, and look at the anguish that's in him, he is so lonely.

Another reason is that the middle class, seeing its opportunity to dominate all American society, pushes its dominance. No matter how much ground the middle class is able to control, it is never satisfied. As soon as an artist appears, and shows promise, the middle class perks up, and if he says anything against them will ridicule him as they did Ginsberg. On the other hand, if the poet shows any tendency to merge with the middle-class values, they will heap honors of every variety on him.

In the article on Donald Hall, you mentioned that Time *magazine almost killed him in their flattering review of his work.*

Yes, . . . *Time* magazine is a perfect example, and its writers never praise a man unless they think they see something middle class in him, and Don Hall happened to be one of the first poets they praised in the post-war generation. As soon as *Time* praised him everyone said . . . "My God, Don Hall must be weaker than I thought he was . . . if *Time* magazine saw something in him."

Ginsberg became a fall guy for the middle class also. Because he had certain extreme tendencies in his person-ality, the middle class was able to call him a nonartist. They tried to absorb him negatively, as opposed to those they absorb positively with prizes, and State Department trips. The only artist they cannot handle, really belongs to the third group of artists who live relatively apart, and try to preserve a certain solitude. Salinger, for ex-ample, offended *Time* magazine. He refused to allow them to come and do a cover portrait of him, or to inter-view him . . . he has a ten foot wall and he puts dogs on *Time* magazine people when they come. *Time* went along with this for a little while until they saw that he meant it, and at this point they became ferocious, and they have cut him to shreds in every notice since then . . . a really naked example of what happens when an American artist refuses to go along with the journalistic middle class.

Why is it that the middle class in America is trying to absorb its poets? You mentioned that it couldn't bear to be ridiculed or hurt. But they must see that he can do nothing for them or for himself when he is a part of them . . . .

Why can't the middle class be content to live by itself and see another group of people living over here with a different group of ideas? Well . . . .

FM: The first thing is that they are not big enough. And secondly, they are too busy rising out of the lower class and the lower middle class to let anything dangerous get near them . . . they are all busy aspiring . . . "Look, this is what you are doing," but he says, "This is what you didn't do."

Yes, it is true that they have great doubts about the rightness of the course they are pursuing; they are not sure that it is right to live only for money, to climb on the backs of other people. When a writer comes along and says the point of life is something totally different, it doesn't matter if he says it in a soft voice, or in a loud voice . . . a terrible anxiety comes in. The only time that people in power and artists help each other, and there aren't many of those periods, is when neither had doubts about the value of what he was doing. There have been governing classes who were proud of themselves.

To escape the middle class you said the poet had to find

a secret life, an inner door to solitude. If this is so, then there never really can be an image of the American poet, because each poet will find his own way.

Yes, but eventually traits in common will develop. From what many American poets have in common, we will finally draw an image of what an American poet is, and I think that is coming. I think it is going to have something to do with men like Stafford, who are able to live in this country with a certain gentleness. I think the connection between poets and gentleness will appear in the United States as well as the connection of the poet and the inward. In South America, because of the battle between the rich and the poor, they see a poet as someone who fights firmly against the rich, and so against the United States, which is always on the side of the rich. Their poets have produced magnificent poetry in this century. In the United States the issues aren't clearly drawn, so the United States poet has to feel his way like a blind man along the wall. However, there is no evidence that poetic power in the United States is declining and becoming feeble. Not at all . . . it is expanding. England by contrast, has a clear idea of what a poet is, but it is not able to pull up creative power to live up to it any more. In America we have much creative power, but we don't know what to live up to . . . .

FM: It could be too that, in time to come, the clearest voices may come out of places like Kansas, provided that that five-foot-deep sea of sensitivity you spoke of has rolled on and come to Kansas.

Harold Rosenberg, the art critic in New York, had a wonderful essay called "French Silence and American

Silence." Suppose the young French poet wants to write a love poem to a girl. Rosenberg says that his mind is so full of poems from the past that every time he sees his girl naked he sees her as a woman naked in a whole shower room full of naked women. He is hardly able to pick out his own because there are so many other literary women. He can write a poem to a woman then very easily, but it might be for many of the other women in the room. His problem is to shut off all those other literary images of women. To put it in terms of sound, going through his head all the time, there's a phonograph record with endless poems in it. What he has to do, and at tremendous will, is to shut his ears so that he hears no sound but that of his own. The American problem is entirely different. The American poet sits on a fence in Nebraska. All around him he hears silence. The American poet cannot even see his girl naked. He sees a woman with a lot of clothes on. In other words, the woman in America has not been described in literature. He does not know how to begin to describe a woman because everything is silence.

FM: I think that if there was a woman out there, it would probably be a scarecrow in the neighbor's field keeping away the crows.

Leslie Fieldler, in his book *Life and Death in the American Novel* has gone over all American novels and has pointed out that there are almost no believable women in them. It is the first time anyone has done that, and the finality of it is crushing. He points out that there are no living women in Melville or Cooper. When you come to Hemingway, unreal women. *A Farewell to Arms* is a marvelous piece but some critics feel it is weakened badly by the love story at the end, which at one time was regarded as the glory of the book. The more you look at it, the more you realize the woman is not real. There are no real women in Hemingway, but there are real men. Anyway, Fiedler draws the conclusion that all American men are homosexual. He hurriedly reports, . . . "I have six children, . . . nine children, no ten!" Every where he looks he sees homosexuality. *The Sixties* published a parody on Fiedler. We called it *"Churchill's History of the English Speaking People* As It Would Have Been Reviewed by Leslie Fiedler." "Well, this is a good book, I guess, but some things about it worry me. How come there are so many men in the book? You know King Henry the V is a man? You realize King Henry VI is a man? Cardinal Newman is a man, how come? . . . And these men are constantly going out in the field, together, sometimes 5,000 of them. Why didn't they bring their wives with them?"

Homosexuality is not the answer. It's more likely that when men write novels, they can just look in a mirror and they can describe an American man fairly well, but it is harder to describe someone different—an American woman.

A woman, then, by the same token should be able to look in the mirror and describe a woman. Why are there so few women writers and poets?

Different answers are given to this question every hundred years, but one good answer says that a woman can create a human, a baby, inside herself. Therefore she already has a connection with the universe. Man, not being able to have babies, creates art. A work of art makes a connection with the universe; so art is a masculine thing by its very nature. The corresponding question is, Why don't men have wombs? But . . . Emily Dickinson was a marvelous poet, and Marianne Moore was a good poet, and Denise Levertov is a very fine poet, and so by no means are there no great writers among women.

FM: It is interesting that the successful women novelists are very masculine. For example, Willa Cather and George Eliot.

When you look at women novelists there is a feeling that not only have they become masculine, but somehow they have deliberately put aside that part of themselves that could produce babies.

Earlier you used an analogy in which you referred to the French poets as taking a long sea voyage, while the Americans seem to be more or less stranded on the land. You said that the French had a kindness and gentleness that the Americans wouldn't allow themselves to have. Instead they have tried to be tough. Why do Americans feel they have to be tough, instead of kind and gentle?

Well, the whole drive of American culture is toward a sort of brutal masculinity. All you have to do is listen to the "Ballad of the Green Berets." I have recently been putting together a booklet called "A Poetry Reading Against the Vietnam War." We have been doing some read-ins and are now printing up the poems various people have suggested. I found an interesting contrast. Winfield Townley Scott wrote "The American Sailor with the Japanese Skull." He describes a sailor who picked up a skull in Saipan. He skinned it, taking the meat off the face and the hair off the head. Then he dragged it behind his ship for about two weeks, and treated it with lye until it was a good clean skull. Now he keeps it in his house. That makes one think of our relationship now to the Vietnamese. This poem is followed by a Walt Whitman poem, in which he says, "My enemy is dead, a man divine as myself is dead. / I look where he lies white-faced and still in the coffin / I draw near, bend down and touch lightly with my lips the white face in the coffin." What a difference in the view of the enemy. Whitman was fighting against the tendency toward brutality in American life. What is so magnificent about Whitman is the gentleness and sweetness—this reconciliation and forgiveness inside of him. In every human being there is a man and a woman, present, hidden, in the genes. The American culture teaches the male to crush and suppress the woman inside of him. What we see in the typical football player is a man who has crushed everything feminine in him and has allowed only the masculine to live. He mistreats women, because he has always mistreated the woman that is inside him. Once he has crushed the feminine part of himself, he becomes unstable. A homosexual is a man who evidently leaves only the feminine part and so he becomes unstable. It is a serious question whether the American football player that everyone admires or the homosexual is the more unstable . . . they are both equally unstable.

The "voyaging" French poet allows the feminine part of himself to live in so far as it is there. The feminine part is responsible for the gentleness and the forgiveness in his poems and what we recognize instantly in literature when we see it—love.

What do you think the American woman has done with her half-feminine, half-masculine self?

Well, the American woman could not help but be affected by the drive toward masculine brutality—I guess she also stamps out some of the womanliness in her. Womanliness is not hated in France, but then neither is masculinity. The French woman does not suppress her masculinity—she is sometimes an amazing creature. I am not saying that France is a better country—I am saying that France does not have our peculiar hatred of womanliness. That all began here with the Puritans—the Christian belief that "sex is evil"—rephrase that a little while and you will soon have "women are evil."

You mentioned the read-ins against the war in Vietnam. Would you tell us something about them?

The first read-in was held in New York in February. It was moderated by Stanley Kaufmann, drama critic of the *New York Times*. About forty people in New York, much respected in literary circles, read for about five minutes each,—reading anything which expressed their feelings. Shortly after, I was about to leave for Oregon to do some readings and I sent a letter ahead to David Ray, who teaches at Reed College, and suggested a read-in at Reed College. When I got out there he had made preparations, and Portland State College agreed! Each college provided money for airfares. We flew in Ferlinghetti, Peterson, Hitchcock, and Logan from San Francisco, and Wright from New York. They would get no fees but would get their air expenses. We did the read-ins at Reed and Portland, and then at the University of Washington. Our idea was simply to take the public read-in and transfer it to the college campuses, having a smaller group of poets in a concerted program which would concentrate on the war. The *New York Times* carried an article on the Portland readings; a good one.

As a result many people in the East also planned similar readings; we started a group called "The American Writers Against the Vietnam War" which included people who had read at Oregon and a few others who were interested. The next read-ins we organized were in Milwaukee and Chicago in the middle of April. More read-ins will take place in the East the first ten days of May, at Harvard, N.Y.U., Columbia, Oberlin, Cornell, and several other colleges in New York State. Some days we will do three readings, going from one college to another. Finally, there will be a huge read-in in Philadelphia on about the eighth or ninth of May. We will then come to Minnesota and have a read-in in St. Cloud on the fourteenth of May and in Minneapolis on the evening of the same day.

What we had hoped would take place did—namely, the idea has spread and many colleges are now planning their own readings, putting them together with poets living nearby. I think it is a healthy thing. Not all the poets feel able to write a political poem and yet most of them are violently opposed to the war. The read-ins give them the opportunity to testify that they are against the war; they can read poems of Jeffers or Cummings or passages from Thoreau. It enables the intellectual community in America to testify to some of their feelings. Some of the poets are writing poems about the Vietnam war and are able to read their own poems. Simpson has an excellent new poem. I think it is good for the students too because they go and for an hour and a half they have to think about Vietnam. They also have a chance to think about the relationship that is possible between poetry and large national issues, such as this war.

FM: Did you ever read Psalm 137?

Go ahead and read it.

FM: No, I just mean you should read it some time. It's a beautiful poem. After all, you are being interviewed, not me. . . .

Please—

FM:

> By the rivers of Babylon, there we sat down, yea, we wept, when we remembered Zion.
> We hanged our harps upon the willows in the midst thereof.
> For there they that carried us away captive required of us a song; and they that wasted us required of us mirth, saying, Sing us one of the songs of Zion.
> How shall we sing the Lord's song in a strange land?
> If I forget thee, O Jerusalem, let my right hand forget her cunning.
> If I do not remember thee, let my tongue cleave to the roof of my mouth; if I prefer not Jerusalem above my chief joy.

[Mr. Bly requested that our interview end with this psalm.]

II

On the War and
Political Poems

On Government Support for the Arts

An Interview with N. G. Schuessler

Dayton, Ohio, Spring 1971

You were one of the founding members of The American Poets Against the Vietnam War. Could you tell us just what this organization has done since its conception?

We go back to a time in 1966, or so, in which Americans were troubled about the war, but everyone was urging them to be cheerful. If you said anything against the war, you were a traitor. The college students were equally confused about it. Most professors would not take a stand. They would have a discussion series on the Vietnam war in which one professor would take one side, the pro-war, and the other take the other side. They would try to present both sides to the students. But the students were not satisfied with that. First of all, it is a passionate issue. They didn't want to hear the professors talking in modulated tones about burning babies. Everyone could see a need in the colleges for some adult to stand up and say the thing is horrible, stupid, and disgusting and revolting, and is against everything you've read in every serious book. One of the things we did was simply gather a group of poets who we knew were opposed to the war. We would go onto a campus and give a Vietnam poetry reading. The first one we gave had about eight or nine poets—Ferlinghetti, Jim Wright, and many others. We presented an hour and a half of poems about the war. Instead of talking about it intellectually, we talked about it at the gut level. When we first started, maybe 10 percent of the students were with us and the other 90 percent against us—booing, screaming, howling. Now, of course, it's the other way around, so we don't do so much of it anymore. We may do a few in the South where they still throw rocks at you.

Often times it's said that poetry with a specific social theme, such as the Vietnam war, loses something in that it gets dated. How would you answer something like that?

You can never answer a question without looking at the assumption underneath it. The assumption underneath this one is a new critical one. It is that poetry is written for posterity, and it must be as good a hundred years from now as it is good now. Who made that rule? Who made that rule? Williams said:

> I am not writing for posterity. I don't care if they read it after I'm dead. What do I care? I'm writing for the people alive in my time; I'd like to move them. I don't care about these people coming. They can get their own poets. I want to move the people alive in my time and one way to move them is to talk about things that move them. And to do that, you often have to mention these things.

There are sudden accidents, you see, like "Macbeth." Shakespeare, for example, is taught as a universal poet, but the best teacher I ever had on Shakespeare was an old man who is still alive in Iowa. He was interested in Shakespeare as a writer of the time. One of the things he proved to me is that "Macbeth" was written as an attack on James the First. The main image of that play is a king whose clothes are too big for him. Suppose you're attacking Johnson and you're having a play portraying Johnson. Suppose that the way Johnson got to be president was by meeting three witches in the woods. That's scary.

Like "MacBird"?

Yes, "MacBird" picked up some of that. But you see, the idea is that Shakespeare was doing a direct, physical, political attack in his time for the people alive in his time. It happened that the play had a lot of other things in it, so it survived and went on. I'm not convinced that he cared one way or another. As you know, when he got sick of it he just said, "I'm quitting. I'm going back to Stratford. Don't bother me."

You once refused a government grant for $5,000. Are you opposed to government grants for the arts in general, or was this specifically because the government was involved in the war at that time?

I think these are separate questions. First, whether a decent government offering prizes to artists is a good thing. Sweden, for example, has lifetime salaries for its writers beginning at the age of thirty-two. If they prove themselves by thirty-two, there is a salary for the rest of their lives. Now, whether that is really a good thing, you know, physically and spiritually for the writer is a different proposition. But that issue didn't come up here. Here, you have a indecent, immoral government murdering people. Then it has the gall to set itself up and say, "We have so much honor. Let us give some of our honor." Do you understand? That dishonorable government has no honor to give. And just the money doesn't make any difference. So I was also making a protest against those writers who did accept it.

You mentioned the Swedish system and questioned whether or not this was desirable. What would be some of the drawbacks of an artist being paid by the government?

That is a good question. I think that there are two entire streams of human life. There is a stream that goes through business and goes through government and goes in a conventional way. Then, there is another stream that Blake represented as a rebellious stream, a stream interested in the inner life of people, not in whether they make money. Now the artist is almost always in this second stream. It isn't that he attacks the government; it's the fact that he is committed to a different style of life than those in the other stream. And they are both needed by the human soul to keep the balance there. You have got to have the artists, the musicians, and these people that keep alive those possibilities of the human soul that would obviously die in IBM. It goes along like this, and Blake was very conscious of it. The state is a killer; the state will destroy art; Rome destroyed all art, etc. All of his work is connected with the tension between these two streams, and he put himself firmly in the second stream. Now, suppose that they're going along like this, and then the state builds a channel between the two streams and the artist looks over. Instead of getting his money from the readers who buy his books—who are also in that stream—instead, he gets it from the government. He gets a link with this stream; maybe he goes over to this stream. Maybe they eventually are able to pull all the artists over to this stream and the other stream dies completely. That is the danger, and I, myself, am opposed. Right now, I'm opposed to all government grants to magazines. They don't intend to soften their criticism of the government. But it happens, it happens. They say, "Well, it can't be so bad if it gave me money. It can't be so bad." I would rather have this firm division here, even if the little magazine suffers. My own magazine never had any money from outside. My wife did the work; I did the work. We got through; we survived. I think it is possible to have little magazines like that going. And they are a great help precisely because they are not helping the government. They are totally independent.

An Argument about "Universal"
versus "Political" Art

An Interview with Gregory Fitz Gerald and
William Heyen

Brockport, New York, Spring, 1970

*Gregory Fitz Gerald: Galway Kinnell said that "Small-
Boned Bodies" gave a new dimension of feeling to war
poetry. To what extent did you have the Vietnam war
specifically in mind?*

It was written after hearing, on radio and television,
Pentagon "counts" of North Vietnamese bodies found.

*G. F. G.: A number of critics and poets regard any poem
which deals with a political subject as propagandistic. To
what extent do you think that's true?*

That is a popular opinion in English departments, and
among British poets and critics. I heard it the other day
from an Irish poet named Richard Weber, who declared
that no poem on the Vietnam war could be any good.
I think the Americans and the British tend to diverge
widely on this issue, and I have a new idea why they do.

The Americans and the British believe that the expe-
rience of love has a psychic origin and so they both find
love poems to be natural. But the English believe that war
has an economic origin. Americans for the first time are

learning that war has psychic sources also. The British, holding to the idea that war rises from economic factors, feel it alien to their own psyche, and believing that, find war poems objective, journalistic, and exterior. England had Vietnams in the nineteenth century and the poets said nothing. Of course the media coverage was very different at that time and so what was done wasn't so apparent. But it's very interesting that during the nineteenth century, virtually no English poet, except Blake, took any kind of stand against the "police" actions that the British Empire specialized in. Tennyson, for example, could happily write a poem about how marvelous it was when five hundred soldiers charged in Crimea, following an English general with bad judgment, and got killed. And this silence, or outright approval, extended to domestic policies as well. All the time that Keats was declaring "Beauty is truth, truth beauty, / that is all ye know on earth, and all ye need to know"—all of that time smoke was destroying grass and trees in the midlands. Six-year-old children were at work and dying in the mines. Why doesn't Keats mention those things? His statement is true, but it is also true that "ugliness is truth, and truth ugliness." So the English have a built-in pact, going way back, by which the poets agree not to mention unpleasant subjects. If you ask Keats about mine children, he might say in effect: "These problems of cruelty to children have an economic origin, and therefore, how can I bring them into my 'Ode to Psyche'?" The war has taught us that not only the Vietnam war, but quite possibly all wars, have their sources inside us.

William Heyen: Would you say we've gone a little bit too far in our worry about this business of "aesthetic distance" these days? Was that just kind of a hedge against the kind of involvement that we have . . .

What is "aesthetic distance"?

W. H.: When Anthony Hecht was here, I asked him why the poems in his last book, The Hard Hours, *were about the Second World War and there were no poems about the Vietnam war, and that's the phrase that comes up. It's an Eliot doctrine.*

A major human problem is that human beings do not live in the present—they live psychically in the past, or in the future. During meditation or "sitting," the sitter is encouraged to live in the present. He does that by keeping his awareness that at this moment he is sitting. It's possible that absorption in the past, uselessly drains our energy. All attempts to live in the future, in "wantings," drain our energy. Literary theorists that call for aesthetic distance by which they sometimes mean fifteen years between yourself and a war before you write about it, merely illustrate the western intelligence's longing to live in the past.

W. H.: Is this our country's problem today?

The fact that we did pay attention to the Negro slums early, when we knew that they existed, in the forties and the fifties, when the migration was heavy, is a perfect example of the inability of white Americans to face the present. Everyone pretended Chicago was "hog-butcher for the world." We notice that whenever an American President wants to bomb, he starts talking in the language of Abraham Lincoln. He wants to act in the present, while living mentally in the past.

W. H.: You still have to worry, though, about the poem not becoming too shrill, don't you? You still have to remember that it's an art form.

80

A poem should be a matter of thought, not of opinion. It's possible to think about a war.

G. F. G.: Do you feel that a poem about warfare touches a universal chord?

I dislike intensely phrases like "universal chord." The English departments keep urging "the universal" in literature, until finally the student poet ends up writing only about his childhood—or some universal subject, such as the labyrinth. "Universal" apparently means the unborn should be able to grasp it too, so the university influenced writer feels above all local conflicts and writes for posterity. That is living in the future again.

W. H.: You used a minute ago a phrase something like the "psychic impulse" or the "psychic energy" of America. In reading your work, I get this sense of fatality. You know, the country being settled by murderers riding under the canvas of Conestoga wagons. And I was reading Hector St. John Crevecouer who said that it was the most vicious of our people who broke the frontier, settled the country. And yet, in your work, there's a tension because I think you move toward affirmation. You move toward the light around the body.

I see the contradiction you're talking about. I do think that despite the brutality everywhere energies involving light are rising in this country. A mood of spirit and love comes close. So apparently, whenever destructive energy increases, the spiritual energies also increase. Hölderlin said, "When the danger is greatest, the saving power also increases." But it is interesting that though the destructive energies affect the country as a whole, and everyone in it, the spiritual risings affect only individual people, and not all of them. You can hear a significant tenderness in the last fifteen years in some rock music, and in the amazing flowering of poetry among high school and college students. But this tenderness doesn't seem to affect the general mood of the country. The country's mood remains brutal. But an American, if he or she works hard, feels doors opening inside. I think you sense my poetry to be affirmative because I recognize those doors; I have felt them. Only a few people felt those doors in the nineteenth century in the United States. Now thousands feel them.

W. H.: At your readings, you're always sounding the dark truths. And many of us listening are grimacing and are hurt. Yet of all the poets I've ever heard, you establish the sense of community and love during your readings.

Thank you.

Edited from a videotape interview with Robert Bly in the Spring, 1970, sponsored by the Brockport Writers Forum, Department of English, State University College, Brockport, N.Y. 14420 © State University of New York.

On Urging Others to Refuse the Draft

An Interview

Amherst, Massachusetts

Last year, when you received the National Book Award, you turned the money over to the New York Resistance. How did your views on the war in Vietnam lead you to do this?

Some years ago I had written a book of poems called *Poems for the Ascension of J. P. Morgan.* But no one wanted to publish that book because political poems were not very popular at that time.

As the war in Vietnam went on and on, I began writing poems about that. I was interested in where it came from inside us.

Then the Resistance began and students started to refuse the draft. Some people, like Spock and Mitchell Goodman and others who were doing draft counseling, felt uneasy because they didn't face any risk themselves. David MacReynolds, one of the leaders of the war resistance in New York, said that he never counseled anyone because the young man was faced with five years in prison and he himself wouldn't get anything.

There was a draft card turn-in at Washington the day before the March on the Pentagon. Cards came in from all over the country—200 cards came from L. A., many from Chicago. Older people accepted cards at the door of the Justice Department. Mitchell Goodman was there. Those of us over draft age also turned in our draft cards. There was a law against it, with a $10,000 fine. The FBI was very fast, and before I got home there was an agent waiting in my living room. They had already been opening my mail for a long time anyway because of my antiwar poetry and organization of readings.

Because of this draft card turn-in, Mitchell who had brought the box of cards into the building and four others were indicted. The purpose of that was clearly to terrify the members of the academic and intellectual community.

It was about this time that some of my antiwar poems came out in a book entitled *The Light Around the Body*. And, by a fluke, it received the National Book Award last year. I intended to refuse the prize but thought that a better use would be to take the $1000 and give it to Resistance. I went down to the Resistance office in New York. I knew some of the workers there. I said, I know how I can get you $1000; and they said, fantastic. I told them the NBA was going to give it to me on Wednesday. One of them should be there to receive the check and I would then counsel him in public. One thought the person should be someone without a beard . . . I didn't think that mattered. Where is it going to be? In Lincoln Center. "We'll have to have somebody with a suit." Then the Resistance member said a sweet thing. "I know somebody with a suit." It turned out to be a young man named Mike Kempton. So Mike called me the next day and I sent him a ticket.

At the end of my short speech, I asked Mike to come up to the stage, gave him the money and counseled him not to go into the army and to use the money to urge others not to go in.

The government had attempted to prevent this public counseling so I thought it a good thing.

When Spock, Coffin, Goodman, Raskin, and Ferber were indicted for conspiracy, do you think that this was actually the first major risk faced by the intellectual community?

Yes, exactly. As a matter of fact, MacReynolds after that said, "Now I feel better about counseling. Now I feel that I can, because I can have the same feeling of risk that he has."

But has the indictment accomplished that?

No, they've been fighting the indictment in the courts. But if Johnson had stayed in, if he had escalated the war by sending in the two hundred thousand more troops as he wanted, I can guarantee that there would be counselors sitting in the clink right now. They have a lot of camps ready and it's obvious that they have been made ready for the intellectuals.

Are you now involved in any new antiwar activities?

We're beginning a series of readings around the country for Resistance beginning April twentieth to the thirtieth, taking in ten cities. We'll be doing this to raise money. Ginsberg has agreed to go along on three readings and perhaps Lowell will join a couple.

During your reading last night you said that we can't do

anything about the war except feel it. Don't you think that is a pessimistic thing to say, when you support resistance and demonstrations?

No. What I was thinking of was people who say to me: "Don't get so excited about the war. It's just going to go on. There's nothing you or anybody else can do to stop it." I mean that the military-industrial thing controlling the war does not intend to be deflected by anything. But, if the resistance becomes strong enough and more students join and the community gets larger, then something can be done. The demonstrations have already gotten rid of Johnson and that was a victory for the peace movement. More victories can come. They can't come along now, though, in an atmosphere where nobody cares enough about the war to act. Everybody's waiting. They expect Nixon to end the war. Our resistance has not been strong enough.

Then you have the problem of people who drop away from the demonstrations because they feel discouraged that the war hasn't ended yet. I was giving a reading in Wisconsin and a student in the audience asked: "How can you go on demonstrating and writing against the war? You've been in jail with Spock, you've done this and that, how can you keep on? I'm nineteen. I've been in the Resistance since I was seventeen and I'm already tired."

So, that's it. We figure we'll do a couple of demonstrations and then the war must end. But in Spain, you understand, students have protested for ten years, fifteen years and they don't expect the regime to end immediately; it's a long range thing and you just keep with it. We have to have more stamina than to fight for only two years.

One of the problems is that people fear that if they take a revolutionary stand now, they will sacrifice their opportunity for a good job or enough to eat.

In other words, they think that there may be another McCarthy era coming. If this is how they feel, then we have lost everything. That is what the Spaniards do not think about. Their jobs are *definitely* going to be taken away. So what—they live with friends and so on. In this country you can live. We shouldn't worry. Even those who lost their jobs during the McCarthy era didn't starve to death. I know it's hard, but we have to realize that we have both the advantages and disadvantages of living in a fantastically rich country. The government should not be able to scare us in this way.

At Brandeis you read a poem based on a theory that a person who dies a violent or distressed death will come back as a ghost. Could you explain this theory and its origin?

This was in a poem called "Driving through Minnesota During the Hanoi Bombings." It goes like this:

> We drive between lakes just turning green;
> Late June. The white turkeys have been moved
> To new grass.
> How long the seconds are in great pain!
> Terror just before death,
> Shoulders torn, shot
> From helicopters, the boy
> Tortured with the telephone generator,
> "I felt sorry for him,
> And blew off his head with a shotgun."
> These instants become crystals,

> Particles
> The grass cannot dissolve. Our own gaiety
> Will end up
> In Asia, and in your cup you will look down
> And see
> Black starfighters.
> We were the ones we intended to bomb!
> Therefore we will have
> To go far away
> To atone
> For the suffering of the stringy-chested
> And the small rice fed ones, quivering
> In the helicopter like wild animals,
> Shot in the chest, taken back to be questioned.

It was the day we bombed Hanoi for the first time, and my wife and I were driving toward Duluth through the beautiful Minnesota fields. I had the feeling that little particles of something were falling in those fields; . . . of grief. As if something permanent, being created by the bombings, were coming to us. Then I remembered a thing that Yeats had said. He said a ghost is someone who has felt intense emotion just before he died. Perhaps some stranger put a knife into him, and he feels that it isn't fair. "It isn't fair! I never saw this man before! It's unjust! It's unjust!" Maybe the most intense emotion he has ever felt. Yeats said that emotion was strong enough to hold his molecules together after his death for a few months or, sometimes, years. He appears and communicates to you. He says, "You wouldn't believe it! I was walking by and this man drove a knife into my back." Suppose you were dropping napalm on some person and the napalm started going up his arm. What kind of emotion do you think this person has? And these emotions are turning into little particles like Uranium 235. And they're dropping all over the United States. It will take a long time for them to dissolve.

I also had the feeling that we wanted twenty-five or thirty years of grief and suffering. We're sick of being happy. That's what we're going to get now, twenty-five years of being unhappy.

On the Lack of Thinking in the Left

An Interview with John Maillett and
Elliot Rockler

Missoula, Montana, Spring, 1975

You were instrumental in organizing poetry readings
against the Vietnam war. What has gone on since then,
specifically with poetry, and generally, the mood of the
country?

I don't know. So many things could be said. I will tell
you a couple of things that I have noticed. One is that
the students never realized how much they had accom-
plished. They didn't realize how much the antiwar pro-
tests really moved the bourgeoise; and they didn't pass
a confidence in that down to the kids in school now.
Also, everything in political life indicates a tremendous
amount of thinking has to be done before you have a
chance to bring down any kind of regime. In some ways
the leftists in America are too feeling oriented—oriented
toward rock music and sort of superficial communities
of their own age group; they never did the thinking that
was necessary. Therefore the whole thing collapsed from
the lack of a real thinking base.

No one really thought out the difference between old
capitalism and new capitalism. They depended on Marx,
who described a quite different situation.

A third thing I've noticed happening is that the students don't feel they can do anything politically.

Every person has a male pole and a female pole. The female pole is placed, so to speak, in feelings and emotions. We don't have to use the words male and female. You can use feeling and thinking, yin and yang, or whatever you want. There is an inner pole and a world pole. Now in about 1968, the students had a very firm world pole. They put it out there and they understood that McNamara was real and that the Vietnamese were real, and that the trains coming in with the recruits were real. Therefore life could spark between those two poles. But their inner pole was very weak. As it turned out many of the leftists, for example, had really very brutal relationships with women. Women got sick of it by the end of the war.

Now something very strange is happening. It is just as if the whole situation were reversed and the pole out in the world is now dissolved. You can find a whole bunch of students and people in their twenties who are working with human relationships and with feeling. They feel that "I'm with the Mother—I love the Mother and I am a feeler." It turns out that they have no relationship with the world at all. This is the pulling into the commune situation in which you ignore all political activity.

I was at a college in Pennsylvania. There are about fifteen hundred students there. One girl told me that she tried to organize a grape boycott, but she couldn't find one student willing to go and pass out pamphlets at the supermarket. Not one student. They don't realize that the world is real.

So there is something fine in the Marxist point of view that the world is absolutely real, and we must keep our pole out there very strongly. One absolutely has to love them for that. But at the same time many of them ignore the soul and spirit.

Their inner pole was very weak,

So you think one of the main reasons that this momentum was lost was because both the thinking and feeling poles weren't developed?

Yes, the leftists did not develop a thinking pole. Another thing is that in spite of everything that is said about the leftists being against the American system, most of them have television sets. And most of them watch television. Television always emphasizes your body, and the fact that you have a frail body, a delicate body. You must feed it correctly and you must cut your underarm hair right and you must do all of these things. That produces a powerful effect. In my opinion what happened at Kent State was that students for the first time realized that the bullets might enter their bodies. And being brought up on capitalist television, they found this a horrifying prospect. They suddenly became afraid. I talked to numerous students who refused to go out after that. They said they might get shot. But from the point of view of the Spanish students who have been struggling for many years, getting shot—what's that amount to? The Spanish students don't have this baby feeling toward their bodies. All of us in America are mothers to our own bodies. And you can feel it. This softness that you feel in the students and in the people who are twenty to thirty to forty years of age. They're always eating just the right kind of vegetables and they always have just the right kind of tea. That's being your own mother.

During the reading you were saying that you like to break down the barriers between yourself and the audience. How successful have you been at that?

There's a strong hunger in the country for something besides television, a hunger for work that talks about the connection between the political and the spiritual—

which talks about a connection between daily life and the political—which talks about the connection between daily life and the spiritual. These audiences are receptive to poetry. They are scared of poetry because they haven't heard it since their high school teacher gave it to them in a puritanical and hatred-filled voice. But if you read poems aloud, they find that they can bring their own experiences forward, and often times considerable life appears in the room.

This was Neruda's experience in Chile. He said to me, "I have visited every town in Chile many, many times. It's very exhausting, but we feel in South America that poetry belongs to everyone and I do this. It's my duty."

You were saying that more and more people hunger for a connection between the spiritual and political. I was trying to think of a system where both coexist, where both are realized in a balanced manner?

Yes, I think the mind has been dominant for so long, for so many centuries that all of our revolutions have failed except for the Chinese revolution. And the Chinese are very careful. They are the ones that have the yin and yang, they will not have the yin without the yang. I think Mao's revolution has succeeded, but it is because he never went through this stupid obsession with only the mind. He insists that the soul be brought forth. Mao spends, what, four hours a day writing poetry? And the spirit is very strong in China, so strong that it can't be wiped out by any number of calisthenics.

Shall I end with a poem? Cesar Vallejo says that true intensity is impossible without intensity of the soul. If you stay in only the political lobe of the brain you have a kind of hysterical intensity, which is not real. The mark is that life lacks some sort of space in it. It is some-how petty. It is like a socialist meeting. Why is it when we know that the emotions behind the socialist passion are so marvelous, then how come the meetings are so boring? Here is Vallejo's poem about intensity.

And what if after so many words,
the word itself doesn't survive!
And what if after so many wings of birds
the stopped bird doesn't survive!
It would be better then, really,
if it were all swallowed up, and let's end it!

To have been born only to live off our own death!
To raise ourselves from the heavens toward the earth
carried up by our own bad luck,
always watching for the moment to put out our
    darkness with our shadow!
It would be better, frankly,
if it were all swallowed up, and the hell with it!

And what if after so much history, we succumb,
not to eternity,
but to these simple things, like being
at home, or starting to bicker with each other.
What if we discover later
all of a sudden, that we are living
to judge by the height of the stars
off a comb and off stains on a handkerchief!
It would be better, really,
if it were all swallowed up, right now!

You'll say that I have a lot
of grief in one eye, and a lot of grief
in the other also, and when they focus
a lot of grief in both . . .
So then! . . . Terrific! . . . So! . . . Don't say a word!

Leaping Up into Political Poetry

An Essay

1

Poems touching on American history are clearly political poems. Most educated people advise that poetry on political subjects should not be attempted. For an intricate painting, we are urged to bring forward our finest awareness. At the same time, we understand that we should leave that awareness behind when we go to examine political acts. Our wise men and wise institutions assure us that national political events are beyond the reach of ordinary, or even extraordinary, human sensitivity.

That habit is not new: Thoreau's friends thought that his writings on nature were very good, but that he was beyond his depth when he protested against the Mexican War. The circumstances surrounding the Austrian Franz Jagerstätter, whose life ended thirty years ago, during the Second World War, are very interesting in this connection. Jagerstätter was a farmer, with the equivalent of a high school education, though he possessed a remarkable intelligence. He decided that the Nazis were incompatible with the best he had seen or read of life, and made this decision before the Nazis took over in Austria; he cast the only "no" ballot in his village against the

Anschluss. Jagerstätter's firm opposition to the Nazi regime is particularly interesting because he did not act out a doctrinaire position of a closely knit group, like the Jehovah's Witnesses, nor was he a member of a group being systematically wiped out, like the Jews: he simply made up his mind on a specific political situation, relying on his own judgment, and what he was able to piece together from the Bible, and using information available to everyone.

When drafted by the Nazis after the Anschluss, he refused to serve. The military judges sympathized, but told him they would have to cut off his head if he did not change his mind. Gordon Zahn's book, *In Solitary Witness,* recounts the meetings Jagerstätter had with various authorities shortly before his execution. All persons in authority who interviewed Jagerstätter, including bishops of the Austrian Catholic church, psychiatrists, lawyers, and judges, told him that his sensibility was advising him wrongly. He was not responsible for acts he might take as a soldier: that was the responsibility of the legal government. They told him that he should turn his sensibility to the precarious situation of his family. He was advised, in effect, not to be serious. It was recommended that he be Christian in regard to his domestic life, but not to his political life. By study Jagerstätter had increased the range of his sensibility, and now this sensibility looked on acts he would have to take under orders by the government with the same calm penetration with which it would look on wasting time, or deciding on the quality of a book. He had extended his awareness farther than society wanted him to, and everyone he met, with the exception of a single parish priest, tried to drive it back again. Jagerstätter, however, refused to change his mind, would not enter the army despite disturbed appeals by the authorities, and was executed.

Most Americans had serious doubts about the morality of the Vietnam war. We are all aware of the large number of spirited and courageous young Americans in the Resistance who refused induction and risked and were given lengthy prison sentences. The majority of American draftees, however, went into the Army as they were told. Their doubt is interrupted on its way, and does not continue forward to end in an act, as Jagerstätter's doubt did or as the objector's and resister's doubt does. This failure to carry through means essentially that American culture has succeeded in killing some sensibilities. In order to take the rebellious and responsible action, the man thinking must be able to establish firm reasons for it; and in order to imagine those reasons, his awareness must have grown, over years, finer and finer. The "invisible organs of government," schools, broadcasting houses, orthodox churches, move to kill the awareness. The schools emphasize competitiveness over compassion; television and advertising do their part in numbing the sensibilities. Killing awareness is easier than killing the man later for a firm act.

2

The calculated effort of a society to kill awareness helps explain why so few citizens take rebellious actions. But I'm not sure it explains why so few American poets have written political poems. A poem can be a political act, but it has not been so far at least an illegal act. Moreover, since much of the poet's energy goes toward extending his awareness, he is immune to the more gross effects of brainwashing. Why then have so few American poems penetrated to any reality in our political life? I think one reason is that political concerns and inward concerns have always been regarded in our tradition as opposites, even incompatibles. *Time* is very upset that Buddhists should take part in political activity: the *Time* writers are convinced that the worlds are two mutually exclusive worlds, and if you work in one, you are excused from working in the other. English and American poets have adopted this schemata also, and poets in the fifties felt that in *not* writing anything political, they were doing something meritorious. It's clear that many of the events that create our foreign relations and our domestic relations come from more or less hidden impulses in the American psyche. It's also clear I think that some sort of husk has grown around that psyche, so that in the fifties we could not look into it or did not. The Negroes and the Vietnam war have worn the husk thin in a couple of places now. But if that is so, then the poet's main job is to penetrate that husk around the American psyche, and since that psyche is inside *him* too, the writing of political poetry is like the writing of personal poetry, a sudden drive by the poet inward.

As a matter of fact, we notice that it has been inward poets, Robert Duncan, Denise Levertov, and Galway Kinnell, who have written the best poems about the Vietnam war.

When a poet succeeds in driving part way inward, he often develops new energy that carries him on through the polished husk of the inner psyche that deflects most citizens or poets. Once inside the psyche, he can speak of inward and political things with the same assurance. We can make a statement then that would not have been accepted in the thirties, namely, that what is needed to write good poems about the outward world is inwardness. The political activists in the literary world are wrong—they try to force political poetry out of poets by pushing them more deeply into events, making them feel guilt if they don't abandon privacy. But the truth is that the political poem comes out of the deepest privacy.

3

Let me continue a minute with the comparison of the political poem with the personal poem. I'll use Yeats's marvellous word *entangle*; he suggested that the symbolist poem entangles some substance from the divine world in its words. Similarly a great personal poet like Villon entangles some of the private substance of his life in his language so well that hundreds of years later it still remains embedded. The subject of personal poetry is often spiritual growth, or the absence of it.

The dominant poem in American literature has always been the personal poem. John Crowe Ransom, for instance, wrote an elegant version of the personal poem, Randall Jarrell a flabby version, Robert Lowell a harsh version, Reed Whittemore a funny version, W. D. Snodgrass a whining version, and Robert Creeley a laconic one, etc. I love the work of many of these poets, but they choose, on the whole, not to go beyond the boundaries of the personal poem. Many poets say flatly—and proudly—that they are "not political." If a tree said that, I would find it more convincing than when a man says it. I think it is conceivable that a tree could report that it grew just as well in the Johnson administration as in the Kennedy administration or the Lincoln administration. But a modern man's spiritual life and his growth are increasingly sensitive to the tone and content of a regime. A man of draft age will find that his life itself depends on the political content of an administration. So these poets' assertion of independence, I think, is a fiction.

The only body of political poetry written with any determination in the United States were those written during the thirties by Edwin Rolfe, Sol Funaroff, Kenneth Fearing, among others. It is interesting that their poems were usually political in *opinions*. For example, the poet might declare that he had discovered who the phonies in the world are, something he didn't know before. But changes of opinion are steps in the growth of the poet's personality, they are events in his psychic history. These "political" poems of the thirties then were not really political poems at all, but personal poems appearing under another guise.

We find many political poems composed entirely of opinions; they are political but not poems. Here is an example from a Scandinavian anthology:

> Poor America
> so huge, so strong, so afraid.
> afraid in Guatamala,
> afraid in Congo, Panama,
> afraid in Cuba, in Santo Domingo,
> afraid in Vietnam . . .
> America, take your hands off Vietnam!
> The poor are rising
> You are through stealing now
> Your face is distorted with hate . . .

These lines have boiled off the outermost layer of the brain. The poem is not inside the poet's own life, let alone inside this nation's life.

The life of the nation can be imagined also not as something deep inside our psyche, but as a psyche larger than the psyche of anyone living, a larger sphere, floating above everyone. In order for the poet to write a true political poem, he has to be able to have such a grasp of his own concerns that he can leave them for a while, and then leap up into this other psyche. He wanders about there a while, and as he returns he brings back plant seeds that have stuck to his clothes, some inhabitants of this curious sphere, which he then tries to keep alive with his own psychic body.

Some poets try to write political poems impelled by hatred, or fear. But these emotions are heavy, they affect the gravity of the body. What the poet needs to get up that far and bring back something are great leaps of the imagination.

A true political poem is a quarrel with ourselves, and the rhetoric is as harmful in that sort of poem as in the personal poem. The true political poem does not order us either to take any specific acts: like the personal poem, it moves to deepen awareness.

Thinking of the rarity of the political poem in the United States, another image comes to mind. We can imagine Americans inside a sphere, like those sad men in Bosch's "Garden of Earthly Delights." The clear glass is the limit of the ego. We float inside it. Around us there are worlds of energy, but we are unable to describe them in words, because we are unable to get out of our own egos.

4

The political poem needs an especially fragrant language. Neruda's "The Dictators" has that curious fragrance that comes from its words brushing unknown parts of the psyche. It seems to me a masterpiece of the political poem:

An odor has remained among the sugar cane:
A mixture of blood and body, a penetrating
Petal that brings nausea.
Between the coconut palms the graves are full
Of ruined bones, of speechless death-rattles.
A delicate underling converses
With glasses, braid collars, and cords of gold.
The tiny palace gleams like a watch
And the rapid laughs with gloves on
Cross the corridors at times
And join the dead voices
And the blue mouths freshly buried.
The weeping is hidden like a water-plant
Whose seeds fall constantly on the earth
And without light make the great blind leaves to grow.
Hatred has grown scale upon scale,
Blow on blow, in the ghastly water of the swamp,
With a snout full of ooze and silence.

The poem's task is to entangle in the language the psychic substance of a South American country under a dictator. The Spanish original, of course, is much more resonant. But even in the translation, it is clear that Neruda is bringing in unexpected images: "The tiny palace gleams like a watch"—images one would expect in an entirely different sort of poem: "rapid laughs with gloves on." Suddenly a blind plant appears, that reproduces itself by dropping seeds constantly on the ground, shaded by its own huge leaves. This image is complicated, created by a part of the mind inaccessible to hatred, and yet it carries the reality of hatred radiating from dictators into the consciousness with a kind of massive intelligence.

Describing dictators in "The United Fruit Company," Neruda uses for them the image of ordinary houseflies. By contrast, the journalistic mind would tend to describe them as huge and cunning. Whitman was the first true political poet we had in North America. His short poem

"To the States," with which this book opens, has great fragrance in its language as well. "(With gathering murk, with muttering thunder and lambent shoots we all duly awake)".

William Vaughn Moody in 1898 wrote some powerful lines:

> Are we the eagle nation Milton saw
> Mewing its mighty youth,
> Soon to possess the mountain winds of truth,
> And be swift familiar of the sun
> Where aye before God's face his trumpets run?
> Or have we but the talons and the maw,
> And for the abject likeness of our heart
> Shall some less lordly bird be set apart?
> Some gross-billed wader where the swamps are fat?
> Some gorger in the sun? Some prowler with the bat?

His poem was written against United States policy the first time we invaded Cuba. The language at times is remarkably swift and intense, particularly when compared to the hopelessly foggy language of political poetry being written by others at that time.

The political poem in the United States after Whitman and Moody lay dormant until the inventive generation of 1917 came along. It revived with mixed results. Pound demanded that American history enter his *Cantos,* Eliot wrote well, though always of a generalized modern nation, rather than of the United States; Jeffers wrote marvellously, but really was not interested in the United States as a nation at all. In the next generation, Cummings wrote of this country using a sense of superiority as his impulse; he almost never escaped from himself. After Cummings the New Critical mentality, profoundly opposed to any questioning of the white power structure, took over, and the language and strength of political poetry survived only in three men, in Kenneth

Rexroth, Thomas McGrath, and a slightly younger man, David Ignatow. During the forties and fifties most poets kept away from the political poem. In his "Ode For The American Dead in Korea," Thomas McGrath wrote:

> And God (whose sparrows fall aslant his gaze,
> Like grace or confetti) blinks, and he is gone,
> And you are gone . . . But, in another year
> We will mourn you, whose fossil courage fills
> The limestone histories: brave: ignorant: amazed:
> Dead in the rice paddies, dead on the nameless hills.

Rexroth has written beautiful political poems, among them "A Christmas Note For Geraldine Udell." His great common sense and stubborn intelligence helped immensely in keeping the political poem alive.

The new critical influence in poetry began to dim in the middle 1950s, just at the time American's fantastic capacity for aggression and self-delusion began to be palpable like rising water to the beach walker. William Carlos Williams's refusal to ignore political lies was passed on to Allen Ginsberg; Neruda's example began to take hold; Rexroth, McGrath, and Ignatow continued to write well; Ferlinghetti separately wrote his "A Tentative Description of a Dinner Given to Promote the Impeachment of President Eisenhower." Many black poets began to be visible. As the Vietnam war escalated, Robert Duncan wrote several powerful poems on the war. His "Uprising" ends:

> this specter that in the beginning Adams and
> Jefferson feared and knew
> would corrupt the very body of the nation
> and all our sense of our common humanity . . .
> now shines from the eyes of the President
> in the swollen head of the nation.

America is still young herself, and she may become something magnificent and shining, or she may turn, as Rome did, into a black dinosaur, the enemy of every nation in the world who wants to live its own life. In my opinion, that decision has not yet been made.

Acceptance of the National
Book Award for Poetry

March 6, 1968

I am uneasy at a ceremony emphasizing our current high
state of culture. Cultural prizes, traditionally, put writers
to sleep, and even the public. But we don't want to be
asleep any more. Something has happened to me lately:
every time I have glanced at a bookcase in the last few
weeks, the books on killing of the Indians leap out into
my hand. Reading a speech of Andrew Jackson's on the
Indian question the other day—his Second Annual Mes-
sage—I realized that he was the General Westmoreland
of 1830. His speech was like an Administration speech
today. It was another speech recommending murder of
a race as a prudent policy, requiring stamina. Perhaps
this coincidence should not have surprised me, but it
did. It turns out we can put down a revolution as well as
the Russians in Budapest; we can destroy a town as well
as the Germans Lidice—all with our famous unconcern.
As Americans, we have always wanted the life of feel-
ing without the life of suffering. We long for pure light,
constant victory. We have always wanted to avoid suf-
fering, and therefore we are unable to live in the present.
But our hopes for a life of pure light are breaking up. So
many of the books nominated this year—Mr. Kozol's on

education in the slums, Mr. Styron's, Mr. Mumford's, Mr. Rexroth's, Miss Levertov's, Mr. Merwin's—tell us that from now on we will have to live with grief and defeat.

We have some things to be proud of. No one needs to be ashamed of the acts of civil disobedience committed in the tradition of Thoreau. What Dr. Coffin did was magnificent; the fact that Yale University did not do it is what is sad. What Mr. Berrigan did was noble; the fact that the Catholic church did not do it is what is sad. What Mitchell Goodman did here last year was needed and in good taste. The sad thing is that the National Book Committee, in trying to honor those who told the truth last year, should have invited as a speaker Vice-President Humphrey, famous for his lies. Isn't the next step, now that individual people have committed acts of disobedience, for the institutions to take similar acts? What have our universities done to end the war? Nothing. They actually help the war by their defense research. What has the book industry done to end the war? Nothing. What has my own publisher, Harper and Row, done to help end the war? Nothing. In an age of gross and savage crimes by legal governments, the institutions will have to learn responsibility, learn to take their part in preserving the nation, and take their risk by committing acts of disobedience. The book companies can find ways to act like Thoreau, whom they publish. Where were the publishing houses when Dr. Spock and Mr. Goodman and Mr. Raskin—all three writers—were indicted? What the publishing houses do is up to them. It's clear they *can* have an editorial policy: they can refuse to pay taxes.

These concerns are not unconnected to such a ceremony as this. For if the country is dishonored, where will it draw its honor from to give to its writers? I respect the National Book Awards, and I respect the judges, and

I thank them for their generosity. At the same time, I know I am speaking for many, many American poets when I ask this question: since we are murdering a culture in Vietnam at least as fine as our own, have we the right to congratulate ourselves on our cultural magnificence? Isn't that out of place?

You have given me an award for a book that has many poems in it against the war. I thank you for the award. As for the $1000 check, I am turning it over to the draft-resistance movement, specifically to the organization called The Resistance. [Whereupon Mr. Bly handed the check to Mr. Mike Kempton who was representing the Resistance.] I hereby counsel you as a young man not to enter the United States Army, now under any circumstances, and I ask you to use this money I am giving you to find and to counsel other young men, urging them to defy the draft authorities—and not to destroy their spiritual lives by participating in this war.

Three Poems

Post Vietnam

The dead come back home, unfolding their scarlet
    ponchos.
Mist drifts over the thruway approaches.
At dawn the lilies open, the buds
in death-water.
Space between jaws slowly widens,
tongues climb into the sky trailing fire,
arms jerkily unfold from the earth like carpenters' rulers.
African drums roll all night for the Lords of Salt,
and the women with their heads down on motel tables.

The Aeroplane

The black streets go on with biting teeth,
and live wombs open to the salt air.
I sit down and open my book
and go in nine leaps into the air.
The plains rush past under the wounded aeroplane.

Mourning Pablo Neruda

Water is practical,
especially
in August, water
fallen
into the buckets
I carry
to the young willow trees
whose leaves
have been eaten off
by grasshoppers.
Or this jar of water
that lies
next to me
on the carseat
as I drive to my shack.
When I look down,
the seat all around the jar
is dark,
for water doesn't intend
to give,
it gives anyway,
and the jar of water
lies there quivering
as I drive
through a countryside
of granite quarries,
stones soon
to be shaped
into blocks for the dead,

the only thing
they have left
that is theirs.

For the dead remain
inside us, as water
remains
in granite—
hardly at all—
for their job is to go away,
and not come back,
even when we ask them.
But water comes
to us,
it doesn't care
about us, it goes
around us, on the way
to the Minnesota River,
to the Mississippi,
to the Gulf,
always closer
to where
it has to be.
No one lays flowers
on the grave
of water,
for it is not
here,
it is gone.

III

Talk about
Writing Poetry

On Writing Prose Poems

An Interview with Rochelle Ratner

New York, November 1975

What is the point of the prose poem form? How does the writing of a prose poem differ from the way in which other poems are written?

I think that the prose poem appears whenever poetry gets too abstract. The prose poem helps bring the poet back to the physical world.

We see many poems in magazines today with a sort of *mental* physical world. Such poems contain "flowers," "trees," "people," "children". . . but the *body* doesn't actually perceive in that way. The body never sees "children playing" in a playground. The body sees first one child with a blue cap, then it sees a child with a yellow cap, then it sees a child with a snowsuit . . . the body sees detail after detail. An instant later the mind enters and says: "That is children playing." . . .

When a poem contains a lot of plural nouns you know the mind has invaded, and the primitive method of perception has been wiped out. . . .

What is harmful about confessional poetry is not so much that it talks about the personal (which is very brave), but that the *mind* dominates confessional poetry. In all of Anne Sexton's work she never tells us of a single bush that she loves more than any other bush. Berryman's late work talks of trees, not one tree. And the same thing is true of Bertrand Russell's prose. We picked up this tendency to use plurals in high school. In political poetry you have to use generalizations often. The mind has to enter and say Vietnamese are dying, because you cannot see the Vietnamese, you're not there. The terrific danger is the danger of being pulled along in that stream. For me the prose poem is an exercise in moving against "plural consciousness." In the prose poem we see the world is actually made up of one leaf at a time, one Lutheran at a time, one apartment door at a time.

Many of your poems have talked about the idea of the "body". . . .

In medieval and later times people talked a lot about a conflict between body and soul. But I believe that what has happened now is that the mind, as we're talking about it, has become more powerful than either the body or the soul. In Dante's time when people were living *in* the body and *in* the soul, sin was possible (including sexual sin). So Dante's poem is about the feeling of being trapped in a body-soul network, and not being able to get out. I don't think people sin in that way anymore. What we're living in is something that would have to be called a "mind-hell," which Dante didn't know anything about. These days the body is fresh, and the unconscious is fresh, and their freshness can act as a balance to this horrifying mind-hell in which people live. We all get trapped in the mind-hell in high school. The question is what are you going to do? Are you going to describe how horrible it is to be in the mind-hell, and continue to live there? We know what that's like, Kafka described that, he did beautifully with it; but eventually the issue is how to get out of the mind-hell.

I remember your poem about seeing Creeley read for the first time, where you describe him as a crow. Are you creating there your own landscape (as a way of getting out of the mind-hell)?

I don't think of it that way. I feel that every person has an animal lying underneath them. Sometimes I can't see it, but with Creeley I had the overwhelming feeling that somewhere underneath he was a crow. So it wasn't an attempt to create a landscape, but to tell some truth that I felt about him (which wasn't rationalized, but which I felt in my body someplace) . . . that I was in the presence of a crow . . .

The Morning Glory *is dedicated to your oldest daughter, Mary . . .*

She is thirteen. The first prose poem I wrote tried to describe a caterpillar that she brought me when she was three years old. I'll read it.

My Three-Year-Old Daughter Brings Me a Gift

She comes and lays him carefully in my hand—a caterpillar! A yellow stripe along his back, and how hairy! Hairs wave like triumphal plumes as he walks.
Just behind his head, a black something slants back, like a crime, a black memory leaning toward the past.
He is not as beautiful as she thinks: the hair falling over his mouth cannot completely hide his face—two sloping foreheads with an eye between, and an obstinate jaw, made for eating through sleeping things without pain of conscience . . .
Now he rears, looking for another world.

It was the first time that I'd really looked at a caterpillar. Usually I look in my mind when I write. My daughter brought it to me and said it was beautiful, though that was questionable. So I decided to try to describe it. It must have been ten years ago. So the prose poem in a way was a gift she gave me.

Recently you have been translating the Sufi poetry of Rumi and Kabir. It seems to me it's a big jump from translating the Spanish surrealists for a long time to these present translations.

To me it's a step, not a jump. Let's go back again, since we were just talking about "mind." Academic poetry, or abstract poetry, or concrete poetry, to me is mind obsessed. What obsesses it is the organizing mind, not the thinking mind. The organizing mind, the same one that lays out the city streets, can control poetry entirely. Neruda understood that early on. He then moved into his surrealism, in which the unconscious and the body move in and break up that mind organization. When I first read those poems I saw freedom in them . . . freer than any of my poems had ever been, freer of those mind obsessions. It was a great discovery and excitement for me to translate those deep surrealist poems of Neruda, because I was in the presence of freedom for the first time in my life. . . . The old Sufis say "very interesting, but you're still not free." (I don't know what I'm saying now.) They say there are experiences on the other side of Neruda's surrealism, after the mind thing has been broken. They imagine a being inside us which can use the unconscious images as food. It's as if Neruda were taking his images and scattering them on the ground for enormous numbers of elephants to eat. But that way it is dissipated. In the Sufi poems some being comes forward and it consumes this free body energy which you have released, and then that being grows stronger inside of you. When you read such a poem, you feel doors open on all sides. That is marvellous!

When you read such a poem, you feel doors open on all sides.

On "Losing the Road"

An Interview with Peter Martin

Minneapolis, Minnesota, November, 1971

Neruda speaks of the necessity of an "impure poetry."
What do you think he means by that? And do you feel
the same necessity?

I don't think that poetry must be pure or impure. What
Neruda is saying is that he's a Cancer; and that as a Can-
cer he likes all kinds of experiences, all kinds of food, all
kinds of oceans, all kinds of fields. So, what he's saying
is that he came into a poetry that was written primarily
by air types—Libras or Aquarians—and it didn't have
enough gut, enough earth stuff, for him. It made him
uncomfortable. So he wrote Cancer poetry, with many
objects in it. Does that make sense?

Mmhummm [nodding head].

So, all he's saying is that we mustn't restrict poetry in
such a way that it temperamentally cramps anyone.

There are some American poets, like Allen Ginsberg,
who are explicit about sexual concerns in their poetry.
In my reading there are only traces or implications of

sex in your poems. How do you feel about talking about sex?

I believe in trying to bring the joy of sex into a poem, but I'm not sure that involves talking about it.

Yesterday you said, "After talking so much I couldn't write a poem now." Does that fit in with what you've just said?

Psychic energy can be drained by talking. My experience is that when, by means of solitude, the psychic energy is prevented from dispersing, then, after five or six days, the psychic energy takes rhythmic forms.... .

Except for one or two places you never mention your family in your work. Why is that?

Well . . . . It's my business, you know . . . . It's my life.

But some writers feel that in order to get down to a very personal, meaningful level they must deal with their family life.

We try to make up rules for poetry and apply them to all the signs, since we're talking of astrology. But every sign is different. And if you try to make a Pisces write Cancer-object poetry, you're going to destroy him. You try to make a Capricorn, who is a rather secretive type, to become a confessional poet, you're going to destroy him.

Why did you leave the Snowy Fields?

What made you think I left the *Snowy Fields*?

Well, the poems you published in The Light Around the Body *were political, and in a very different style from your earlier book.*

As it happened, I wrote a number of the political poems before I wrote *Snowy Fields,* but they were published later. I write what you call "snowy fields" poems without pause, maybe eight or nine a year. They gradually come along.

In Silence in the Snowy Fields *you wrote, "We know the road." The poem goes:*

1

After many strange thoughts,
Thoughts of distant harbors, and new life,
I came in and found the moonlight lying in the room.

2

Outside it covers the trees like pure sound,
The sound of tower bells, or of water moving under the ice,
The sound of the deaf hearing through the bones of
   their heads.

3

We know the road; as the moonlight
Lifts everything, so in a night like this
The road goes on ahead, it is all clear.

You even entitled that section "Silence on the Roads." Then in The Light Around the Body *you ask, "Where has the road gone?" What is that road you're talking about? Have you found it again?*

The poem in *The Light Around the Body* which asks,

"Where has the road gone?" was written about ten years before the poem that says, "We know the road." Poems are not always published in the order in which they were written!

Yes, but is there any particular reason you had them published in that order?

I couldn't finish the longer one! It's called "The Fire of Despair Has Been Our Saviour," and it goes like this.

Today, autumn.
Heaven's roots are still.
O holy trees, rejoicing ruin of leaves,
How easily we see spring coming in your black branches!
Not like the Middle Ages! Then iron ringing iron
At dawn, chill wringing
The grass, clatter of saddles,
The long flight on borrowed stone
Into the still air sobered by the hidden joy of crows.

Or the Ice Age!
Another child dead,
Turning bone-stacks for bones, sleeves of snow blowing
Down from above, no tracks in the snow, in agony
Man cried out—like the mad hog, pierced, again,
Again, by teeth-spears, who
Grew his horny scales
From sheer despair—instants
Finally leading out of the snowbound valley!

This autumn, I
Cannot find the road
That way: the things that we must grasp,
The signs, are gone, hidden by spring and fall, leaving
A still sky here, a dusk there,
A dry cornleaf in a field; where has the road gone? All
Trace lost, like a ship sinking,
Where what is left and what goes down both bring despair.
Not finding the road, we are slowly pulled down.

I got the first stanza done, the second stanza done, and I could not finish the third stanza in the way I wanted it. Finally, in desperation, I put it into *The Light Around the Body*. I had worked on it ten years, and still the last line isn't any good. I'll do it again. I thought it was all right when I published it, but it isn't. I mean that the sensation of grief is very important in finding the road. In the Middle Ages people studied grief; it was all around, and the road was easier to find then, I think. But now everyone studies cheerfulness. Everyone wants to be cheerful. And so in the end of the poem I am saying that my despair over failure to sense grief is a kind of grief itself. Not finding it . . . you see, I haven't said it yet.

In the essay, "Looking for Dragon Smoke," you said, "A generation of poets is active in Europe and South America. A vast effort is being made once more to open the doors of association. When the poet is in the middle of a poem, about to set down a word, how many worlds is he free to visit?" But earlier in the essay you said that some writers in taking the risks in trusting the unconscious had gone insane. Specifically you mentioned Hölderin, Gerard de Nerval, and Nietzsche. Do you view insanity as a real danger?

No, I don't think so. Members of a democracy generally fear and hate the unconscious, and then men go insane, because of that imbalance. Or is it exploiters who hate the unconscious?

We have a few cases of writers who go the other direction—choose to trust their unconscious all the way, and then have bad luck. But some change has taken place. This is how Jung describes the change.

Let's imagine that the ego is here [indicating a sphere]. It is a self-regulating system. Then unconscious material begins to flow in. Now we can imagine two possibilities. One is that the ego turns, and faces the unconscious material coming in. The ego cannot control its arrival, it can merely observe it. (For example, at a funeral, we often notice perceptions coming in from the unconscious.) The ego then, having had its "threshold" lowered, goes into a depression, which is often the *mark* of new material coming in. Jung says that you can notice this state of depression in writers several thousand years in the west, clearly visible in the poem or story, and always associated with the arrival of new contents. Conrad is an example, so is Catullus; Baudelaire a perfect example. The depression is a *coloring* in his poems; "Flowers of Evil." That's interesting.

But recently something else has begun to happen, on a wide scale. By recently I mean a hundred years or so. We imagine the ego again. The ego sees the unconscious material coming in, only this time it turns its back. It doesn't "think it over," it doesn't try to relate the new material to an ethical system, it doesn't *chew* on it. In the old way the ego went into a depression because it lost the battle with the unconscious material coming in—it tried but was outflanked. It then lost morale—cheerfulness is a sign that the ego is remaining buoyant. In this second "style," the ego does not fight with the perceptions and instinctual memories and repressed personalities coming in. On the contrary, it turns its back, and pretends nothing unusual is happening. As a result, the sphere of the ego begins to get larger and larger. It is just like a balloon being blown up. Jung calls this "spiritual inflation." When this happens to a writer, it affects his literary style. It happened to Nietzsche about the time he wrote *Thus Spake Zarathustra*; the style is hideously archaic, rhetorical, and overblown. I suspect some experience of this sort ruined Ezra Pound's style also, making the *Cantos* unreadable. During the sixties, we saw a lot of poetry of this sort brought on by acid, for acid does bring unconscious material in, and does so while the ego is helpless; so an acid trip is a model for this sort of inflating experience. The person has the sensation he is Rimbaud, he has just had a great revelation. Something like that happens to "Jesus freaks" also. They have the sensation that Jesus guides them to a rooming house. "Jesus told me which room to rent!" He is now a spiritual leader. That sort of inflation is everywhere, now. Everyone in the United States is in danger of it. What is interesting is that Jung said it is a rather new disease. It's not very old. Anyway, that's what Jung describes as spiritual inflation, and it's a kind of insanity that's getting worse. Does that help at all?

Yes, it does.

Two Halves of Life

An Interview with Phil Yannella

Milwaukee, Wisconsin, October 29, 1968

I'd like to go to the question of how a poet grows.

It seems a man's life breaks naturally into two halves. In the first half of his life, up to thirty-five or forty, he spends his energy in strengthening his ego. At about the age of forty, a man makes a great change: he reverses course, and essentially spends the rest of his life trying to make the walls of his ego more porous. He wants to get out of it now, into grass and trees, into others, into darkness, into "the universe." A woman's life apparently divides in this way also, though the change takes place somewhat earlier.

The trouble is, for the most part no one gives us any instruction on how to pass from the first to the second stage. No one ever tells us that such a passage is natural. The whole civilization is dedicated to strengthening the ego, up to the day you die.

We have consequently a contemporary literature that takes place almost entirely inside the human ego. Arthur Miller is a gloomy instance of that; he is still firmly in the first stage. His plays, unlike Greek tragedies, have nothing in them but people. His work is entirely bound to the human plane. Truman Capote and Norman Podhoretz are two more examples of inability to leave the first half of life. Journalism is at home in the first stage. Allen Ginsberg, oddly enough, after a genuine ingression into the second stage—the marvellous interview with him in the *Paris Review* makes it clear how genuine his leap into the "universe world" was—is now returning to the first stage. As he describes it, in that interview also, a voice in India told him "Renounce Blake." That's a rare movement. It's not good for his poetry.

Rilke apparently lived in the second stage from the time he was twenty-four or so. There will is of little importance, complaining is nothing, fame is nothing, openness, patience, receptivity, solitude, is everything. In Rilke you have a genius ten times over who obeyed the laws of what Jung calls the second stage of life.

What you're saying then, Robert, is that after the poet reaches the second stage, the poem sinks in somehow and then blows back out, or comes out.

Yes. Rilke had faith in his natural growth and the faith proved to be perfectly justified. He got out what he had to say and then he died—at forty-nine or so. But I think this business of patience is important for Americans, not only because our poets mature later than Europeans, but also because patience has something to do with images. I mean that you have to be very patient and wait for the images to come. I remember when James Wright was at the University of Minnesota, he'd come out to the farm sometimes, and write poems. And then one day he told me a wonderful thing. He said, "Robert, I put this poem in a drawer two weeks ago, and today I went back and the poem had grown! I swear to God it had gotten larger! That's what to do, put it in a drawer."

Stanley Burnshaw is one of the most intelligent men I have ever met. One day he said, "You know this whole thing of teaching poetry in workshops is wrong. The idea comes across that you can *teach* poetry, *teach* a poet to write. The truth is that for a poet poetry is a natural excretion. Exacly like fingernails, or dung, or hair! That's what it is; and it comes out of a man naturally." Do you ask someone why he grows fingernails? Sometimes a teacher will close the fist, so that the fingernails will grow right into the palm of the hand. Then you have a fist for life. But the problem is to keep your hand open.

Obviously, though, young poets have to read. But aside from people like Whitman and Crane, and maybe even Patchen in some of his poetry, who does the poet go to to help him?

Well, I think he might read the Spaniards and the South Americans poets. And, of course the Chinese. In South America the ocean is sloshing, breaking over onto land. In ancient China you have a very quiet intermixing of the levels of consciousness. It does not lie in layers as water does in a lake in wintertime. Somehow it has all flown around together. The ancient Chinese poetry still seems to me the greatest poetry ever written.

Poetry Is a Dream That
Is Shared with Others

An Interview with Paul Feroe,
Neil Klotz, and Don Lee

Northfield, Minnesota, March, 1973

Mr. Bly, there are some poets that say they go through
a regular routine or regimen to get themselves prepared
to write. Do you have a certain routine that you go
through?

Well. This morning I was looking over some poems for a
book of poems I wrote while I was out in California last
year. Here's one of the little poems:

Nightfall at Pierce Point

The last wisps of sea leap in the feathery sun
  The sedimentary rock settles down for the night
The unconscious of man opens like a flower;
  The sea widens and disappears.

It seems that man's unconscious opens around twi-
light. I don't know if the animals' do this or not, but as
you know clams, even after you take them out of the
sea, continue to open and close according to what the
tides would be. Human beings also do that.

Jung mentions when he visited Africa that all the

drumming and singing in the village would stop at sundown and the villagers would go through an hour or two of depression. Which he understood was connected with the unconscious opening and taking in the fact that night was coming—which also was the suggestion that each would die. This produced a depression for a couple of hours; about eight o'clock or so the drums would start up again and life would go on. We all feel that; the famous cocktail hour is intended to kill that, and cheer people up at dusk. This idea I didn't learn from Jung, but I learned it myself noticing that many of the poems in *Snowy Fields*—my first book—were written at dusk.

It's still true, I write rarely in the morning, which is the time when your conscious mind is most awake. In the afternoon your conscious mind is still awake and then your unconscious mind also opens and joins you. So I ordinarily have some solitude in the morning. I usually sit for a couple of hours before breakfast, from five to seven, and then I spend the morning doing letters. In the afternoon I'm alone until ten at night and do almost all my writing from four until ten or so. It isn't always good, but it's a good time to write.

Does it bother you that you have to be alone to write poetry? You've made the choice to be a writer of poetry and of necessity for yourself to write poetry you have to have solitude. Does that bother you at all?

It happens that I like solitude very much. Now some people find solitude very painful. Hemingway, for example, didn't particularly like solitude. He complained about the terrible loneliness of being a writer; if you lose that solitude then all the writing goes. But it happens that I like solitude—tremendously. The main problem with me is that I would prefer to be with my children and my family more, especially in the afternoons and evenings.

You mentioned in your essay in Sleepers Joining Hands *that when poets are alone and they're happy, then the Ecstatic Mother is with them; one of the four parts of the mother consciousness is helping them along. But if you feel alienated when you're alone or afraid to be alone— you mentioned Beckett—then there's another kind of mother with you. Along with that, what kind of mother do you think is with the so-called alienated writers when they're writing?*

What I call the Teeth Mother—or Stone Mother is probably better. A mother that threatens a part of their unconscious. It is a part of their female unconscious which is threatening them with psychic death all the time.

And they write from fear of psychic death?

It's like a ghost that appears in the room. Some are literally in fear of their psychic lives each time they write. It's clear that experiences like that were behind many things that Kafka and Beckett wrote. But the main idea I am trying to get out is that men cannot write without their woman consciousness being present with them in the room. And if it happens that their woman consciousness is not one of the ecstatic women such as Dante's Beatrice, but instead is a death mother, like Hedda Gabler, or Hemingway's mother, then that person has tremendous pain in solitude, tremendous anxiety all the time. Now think how painful that life is as a writer. You can't write without it, and yet it's always there.

Now that's much closer to Hemingway. Hemingway

in his little short story, *"A Clean Well-Lighted Place,"* talks about how much he wants to stay in a lighted cafe and not go home to that darkness in his room, because he knows that this Death Mother is going to be right there with him. And she finally got him.

Some writers have to revise quite a bit of what they write and some have said that the best things that they write come out whole on the page. First of all, do you do much revising of your poetry, and secondly, along with your view on mother consciousness, do you feel that revision—being more of a critical activity—is more father consciousness than mother consciousness?

Well, the strange thing is that some poems come apparently whole and need very little revision. It's less so when you're just beginning. But many of the poems in *Silence in the Snowy Fields* were written while I was literally sitting under a tree, or in the thirty or forty seconds that it took to write the poem down—and not revised.

The other night, I went out for a walk about midnight. There was a third-week-moon visible in the west, and coming back along the road I noticed my own shadow which wasn't strong like a sun shadow but was a very clear moon shadow slipping along through the little bits of dead weed and grass at the side of the road. And I'd never noticed that before. So I wrote a poem there—three or four lines. I don't know if it's good or not yet. So a poem seems to suggest by something that happens in the outer world in the unconscious. If the unconscious responds and notices it, the poem is there.

So a person writing poetry is always joyful when a poem like that comes along, because he knows that it has come completely without being asked for, and the chances are it's got some freshness in it.

I have many other poems not so clear. The unconscious also responded, but the difference seems to be that if there are any ideas mixed in that stream which is flowing upward, then the poem will probably need a lot of revision. Contrary to rationalists, who believe there are no ideas in the unconscious, I think there *are* ideas, but they are ideas which we have not yet thought through—they're part of our shadow-ideas. When they appear in a poem the easiest thing is to cut them out and return the poem to its sensual base; but the more difficult thing to do is to try to bring the idea in and give it just as much honor as you give the images. In which case you may have to wait two or three years until you have understood the idea with your conscious mind. Then the rewriting takes place.

This happened to me in a poem I started on the night that Johnson was elected years ago, and I still have some work on the final lines of it. It's only about eighteen lines long, but I must have done thirty drafts of it so far and I still have work. There's no question that a poem is a gift of mother consciousness, and the rewriting is done partly with the father consciousness. To some extent— if it's totally done with the father consciousness, you destroy the poem. So the mother has to be there but nevertheless it is the father (in the terms which I was using in that essay) that understands ideas.

You said that poems are less whole at the beginning. Why is that?

It's hard to say why, and it may not be true for people in more primitive cultures where the unconscious is trusted more. But we go through twelve years of school where the teacher teaches us not to trust spontaneity or intuition, but only to trust the conscious mind and the memory. That obviously had a disastrous effect on your relationship with your own unconscious! So when a poet begins writing it is always the same kind of a process. He turns to the unconscious and the unconscious will sometimes respond by giving him one line. Then his conscious mind will fill in the other nine lines of his ten line poem—out of memory of previous poems he has read or what the conscious mind thinks would be the appropriate emotions for this man to have in this situation. Hemingway said you have to write for over ten years before you realize which emotions you have are actually yours. The rest of them are picked up from what you think you ought to feel at that moment.

What the young poet needs at that point is someone who's able to pick out that genuine line—and it'll be the weirdest line in the poem usually, the one that apparently doesn't make sense. But that'll be the line that's coming from his own unconscious; it'll look weird because it's original, because it hasn't been seen in a poem before. Now most editors and most teachers are going to prefer the other nine lines; they'll say, "My, this fits in very well with the tradition of such-and-such and so-and-so." It's very difficult to find that person who can help. When you find that person, it makes you more aware; you're not able to fill in the other nine lines, but you become aware of which line is yours. Maybe in the next poem two lines will be given you by the unconscious. Then you go on in this way until eventually the day comes when an entire poem has all of your own weird lines in it.

Do you feel that all your later poems now are written from the unconscious?

You learn to recognize to some extent the psychic tone

of your own unconscious. And if that psychic tone is not in a line, then I leave it out. I was doing a long poem called "Sleepers Joining Hands"; it has 480 lines in it and I wrote about 5000 lines for it, of which 4500 were written by some other part of me, or my memory—they didn't have the tone! And if I were twenty-five years old, I wouldn't have known what to leave out. I may have left out the wrong things now, but. . . .

At St. Olaf you mentioned that in the poem "Driving Toward the Lac Qui Parle River," you found something that would have been better upon rereading it, but you couldn't change it. . . .

Yes, those lines described driving past fields at night in a car: "This solitude covered with iron / Moves through the fields of night / Penetrated by the noise of crickets."

I wanted to have the sense of the crickets penetrating into the close world of the car, but at the moment I wrote it I made a mistake and said that the solitude is *covered* with iron—which it's not, it's *surrounded* in a circular way; and even worse, the car is not made of iron at all, it's made of steel. I didn't notice that for three to four months until a friend pointed it out to me, and by that time I couldn't change it. The reason is that somehow all the sounds in a given line are chosen by your unconscious and your conscious mind together in a split second, at the very moment that you're also deciding which of the many images possible you will use. Once I chose the word "iron" which has a very heavy, strong *i* in it, this affected the sounds coming in the next line which reflect that *i* and that *r* and that *n* and join or contrast. I went back later and tried to put in the word *steel,* the entire stanza disintegrated in sound, and the lines after it lost all of their sound interest. So I realized that it was too late at this point to change it. There was nothing I could do about it.

You mentioned before the problems of young writers. One of the problems of young writers is said to be that they haven't experienced enough to be able to write good poetry. In your own images, you seem to draw at times on your very specific surroundings—your own farm, Minnesota, things you've seen or attended. Other times your images seem to come from nowhere—from Vietnam or from places you've never been. Do these images come from different places, or do they reflect different ways you feel at a certain time when you write these different images, or do they both come from the same kind of consciousness?

I think it's good to say that psychic life is so mysterious that no one knows where these images come from. But dividing them in this way into sensual details that have been familiar to me since childhood, then another whole set of details come from outside—it's not your personal reality—this division corresponds to some ideas that Jung and others have had. There's the possibility that you have a *personal* unconscious, including memories that are linked with your emotional life; for me those were experiences of seeing trees and farms near our farm, and most of the poems in *Snowy Fields* are written with details like this which have been living in my brain since childhood. Then (though many rationalists don't accept this idea) it's possible that you have another consciousness which links you to the entire community. There's a wonderful speculation by the man who wrote *The Soul of the Ape*, Eugene Maurais. Another of his books is called *The Soul of the White Ant,* and his idea is that an ant colony is not four thousand ants, it's that just as we send nervous impulses out through our flesh and blood, to the tips of our fingers, so the ants at the far edge of the colony pick up the nervous signals that come out from the center of this being. The fact that there's air in between instead of meat is insignificant. Messages can go across air just as well as across meat. So the ant at the edge of the colony, the ant a half mile away from the colony, knows the moment you put a stick into that anthill. That's a very scary and wonderful idea.

Perhaps we are a part of one being, and the images that come in from somewhere else come in from some other people's brains or the brain of some huge being which is—who? I'm sure that's true. I'm sure that the thing that's confusing about dreams is that some dreams come directly from you and others come from other people in your town with whom you share things.

A friend of mine a few months ago—she's rather psychic, and part Cherokee—was sleeping in the room of a strange building. She woke in the night with tremendous palpitations of the heart, difficulty in breathing, pains. Since she was very healthy and had a strong heart she wasn't terribly worried, but it did keep her awake for a half hour and it was very unusual to her. The next morning she found out that the man sleeping in the room through the wall had died at that time from a massive heart attack. The sensations that he was feeling had gone right through the wall into her body and into her brain. So we don't know, but I suspect that some of the images in poems come from similar sources.

You spoke of dreams. Do you remember your dreams and write them down?

Yes. One of the helps for psychic growth that's been used for centuries is study of one's dreams. They appear to have the same function for the human being as that small black navigator's box does for the passenger airplane. This navigator's box picks up when the plane is leaving course, getting too far off to the edge. Your dream is able to tell you when you're going off. There was a new book reviewed in the *Minneapolis Tribune* a couple of weeks ago about a tribe in Brazil (not many in the tribe, several thousand, I think). It's a dream tribe; when they wake up in the morning, the smallest child tells his dream first, then the parents interpret it, then the next oldest, and finally the mother and the father tell their dreams. It takes two hours or so every morning during breakfast, and all the dreams are interpreted. There hasn't been a suicide among the tribe for two hundred years and no violent crimes. Some of the details are terrifically interesting. They encourage the conscious mind to merge with and add to the dream. For example, the child says, "I had a dream last night that I fell off a tree, but just before I hit the ground I woke up." And the father says, "That's a wonderful dream. Now next time you have it, try to stay awake until you hit the ground and see what it's like. I don't think you'll die. See what happens."

Is this the same idea you have in mind when you write your poems. Is that the same as sharing it?

Yes, I think a poem also is a dream, a dream which you are willing to share with the community. It happens a writer often doesn't understand a poem until some months after he's written it—just as a dreamer doesn't understand a dream. And there are people who believe that the purpose of rhythm in a poem, the reason why there is strong rhythm—as in a Yeats poem, as opposed to prose—is precisely to put you into a mood which resembles the brain waves of dreams.

You mentioned that now you can usually recognize your inner voice when you write, whereas the younger poet is just getting to know his voice and he gets perhaps one line out of a poem from it.

I could be mistaken of course, hearing totally the wrong voice.

True, but don't your poems become longer as you become more in touch with your voice? This seems to be the trend in your poetry.

Yes, it also means as poems get longer, you're allowing the intellect to take more part. Intellect in the West, as many people have felt in the last ten years, often has a destructive influence on psychic life. When you find the organized intellectual, the one who is defensive about rationality and intellect, you find a person who is dead spiritually. St. Olaf had lots of professors like that when I was there.

So for the person who writes poetry, the great joy of the poem lies in his or her being able to make an utterance in which the shallow intellect—which has really been trained through grade school and high school to be destructive—doesn't enter. He can continue to write that way the rest of his life if he wishes. Or once he feels that his spontaneous being has been given confidence and is safe from the attacks of rationality—the destructive attacks—then he can choose to ask the intellect to reenter. *Not* on *its* terms, but on the imagination's terms. Blake is just fantastic in this, because he understands that the

educated eye of man

imagination has to be made supreme over the reason or else the civilization dies.

It's strange that when schools read Blake, they read his early poems and say that his later poems are completely incomprehensible or written when he was insane.

Let's see, what are some of his little proverbs about this . . . "Expect poison from standing water." Once the intellect gets in charge through the schools it becomes stagnant. "The roaring of lions, the raging of the stormy sea, the howling of wolves and the destructive sword, are portions of eternity too great for the eye of man." And by the eye of man here he really means the educated eye of man that has been educated through a rational school. It can no longer understand something as magnificent as the roaring of a lion. Only the imagination can understand it.

It seems like there are many ways to become spiritually dead. One is by being too reasonable or rational. The other way is a little bit more mysterious. In "The Teeth Mother Naked at Last" you said that the lies of this country mean that it wants to die. Do you see the country still moving toward this death consciousness?

Maybe the question is: "What are some of the signposts along the way to spiritual death?" Let me ask *you*. Do you see any evidence of any of this movement in St. Olaf? What evidence do you see of a movement toward spiritual death? Or spiritual health?

I would say there is too much emphasis on a system that emphasizes grades.

Why is that?

Grades

I would say because it emphasizes something that's exterior to the real process of learning.

Sometimes competitiveness in the West evidently has a destructive effect on the psyche, and the grading system probably reflects that.

But not only that. The grading system takes the minds of students off things that they should be on. In other words, it's more or less playing a game, a game that occupies you so fully that you need not think about things outside of that system—things in society that should be changed.

Well, what you have suggested here is a fault, if it is a fault, of the *faculty.* How about the students themselves? Do you see any evidence of habits that lead to spiritual death?

I would say that there seems to be a pent-up emotion that's channeled through studying during the week. Then on weekends there's limited release through alcohol or other means exterior to your own self.

Oh, so you think even the release doesn't help, somehow?

It puts you back into the same system. The so-called weekend release itself is a shield from more difficult kinds of thinking or a more serious relation to yourself or with someone else. It's never inward directed, either.

Yes, that's true. A man named Ruuttila wrote to me and said that he felt a genuine response on the St. Olaf campus to the Dick Gregory visit, and to the events at Wounded

Knee, but that he felt it would be hard to sustain this kind of concern on the St. Olaf campus. Why is that?

For some of the reasons we've been mentioning. And also because there isn't that tribal sense of hearing the same drum at the same time. For some reason people walk around and they don't relate. . . . It's almost like we can feel concern for the broken treaties, but not for the condition of the Indians.

It's very mysterious as to why this should be.

It seems that in our way of life the father is the provider, who dishes out desserts as they're merited, whereas the mother accepts everyone.

There was some anger in our little town recently when one of the church study groups read *Bury My Heart at Wounded Knee.* Many conscientious Lutherans refused to feel any guilt toward the Indians at all. A few refused even to read the book, refused to go past the first chapter. The Lutheran Church as a whole is caught in a trap here. The Church continues to declare their pride in their missions although it has become utterly clear in the twentieth century that the foreign missions of the Christian church have been deeply destructive to the psyches of the "native" people. You've surely read the reports of anthropologists—a civilization can be destroyed if its religion is destroyed. The first thing the Christians do is to destroy the "native" person's confidence in his own religion.

A place like St. Olaf then is curiously schizophrenic in that it tries to follow the advances in chemistry and in physics and in literature, but it then has to ignore the discoveries made in anthropology because it wants to be proud of the Lutheran missionaries it helps send to other parts of the world. It seems to me the St. Olaf campus will be ill until the students and the faculty face this issue. The psychic deadness on the St. Olaf campus must be connected with this arrogance.

We've been taught in school that of course primitive people must be inferior or they wouldn't need Christianity. I see no real effort to counteract that among Minnesota Lutherans.

I've been trying to find an answer to Mr. Ruuttilla's question, namely, what practical steps could be taken at St. Olaf to encourage a continuing concern once something like Wounded Knee has passed away. I have one idea. Black Elk, as he says so beautifully in *Black Elk Speaks,* learned that he had to *act out* his dreams and visions. White people might learn to do that too. If it's true that students really are interested in the poor and in the Indians and Blacks, whose main difference from us is that they have less money and less goods, and if Christianity really does say that material things are unimportant, and if St. Olaf *is* a Christian school, then this might be a way of acting out the dream. Every week each St. Olaf student would take some material object that's his or hers such as a hi-fi set, or a hair dryer, or a Luther League pin, or a rock record, or a shirt, and throw one of these into a pile in the center of the campus and see how many weeks he was able to go before he found a material object that he or she really wanted— that he didn't want to throw away. At that point he has hit his limit. At that point he or she has got to expect to be dead. . . .

You said in your speeches that you're impressed with animals and the way animals are able to feel and have their own consciousness. You've spoken about the ants, how there is a real community among them. For me, part of the respect for their feelings is to not to be a cause of their death by continuing to eat meat. Are you a vegetarian?

No. I have from time to time eaten only vegetables, but I'm not a vegetarian. The whole thing has gotten much more complicated lately from the new researches done with lie detectors on plants. Have you followed that? We assumed in the beginning that only human beings had souls and feelings, and therefore we didn't eat human beings. But animals did not have souls. It turns out the more you observe animals, the more you understand that they do have souls. As Lorenz points out, geese feel grief if their goose friend dies. They even get bags under their eyes from grief. But we still maintain that plants do not feel anything. We can eat them all. It turns out from the new research that not only do plants have feelings, but the feelings register on a good lie detector. If you cut a plant, all of the other plants in the room react with very measurable, electrical stimulation. One of the first things the experimenter did was to take a plant, I think it was a philodendron, and put a pot of boiling water near it, and drop in live shrimp. At the moment those shrimp hit the water, the lie detector attached to the plant moved. And he continued to test the sensitivity until he's now found that if you cut your finger in the presence of a plant, the dying red and white cells in your hand will cause that plant to react. So it's exactly as the occult people have said for a long time, that the whole universe is incredibly alive and interconnected.

So if you avoid eating meat, that doesn't mean that you're not a murderer. Men like Ghandi ate vegetables, not for picty, but because they felt a decline in the amount of sheer masculine aggressiveness. That's a more practical issue. And it seems to me that's a strong argument for not eating meat. On the other hand, if a man's doing something that requires a lot of physical aggression, then he should be eating meat. It seems to me the problem with the whole thing is that we each hope we can find some position in which we will be holier without making any terrific amount of effort.

But animals eat other animals. No one knows how it is on other planets, but on this planet it appears that energy is always gained from another living thing. If you use your energy for growth then the animal that you eat will forgive you for eating it. If you use it in some way that attempts, at least, to advance the evolution of all living matter then the lettuce forgives you for eating it, and the deer forgives you for eating it. Blake says in one of his Proverbs of Heaven and Hell, "The cut worm forgives the plow." If the plow is going straight ahead and knows where it's going, the worm forgives it for cutting it in two. But if the plow is just wandering around doing nothing, then the worm will not forgive it.

This is related to the attitude of the American Indians, who as we know are animal eaters, not vegetarians. Yet they have that attitude toward animals which we long to have—the one that you describe—which I represent poorly in my own poems. Before they killed an animal, before they went on a buffalo hunt, they always asked forgiveness of the animal and they would say to the buffalo: "I'm going to have to do this in order that my wife and children will be able to eat this winter, and we do not die. Now this does not mean that I consider myself superior to you or separate from you but I'm going to have to kill you." We don't know what that did for the animals, but it apparently had a deep effect on the psychic life of the Indian.

I heard a story a few months ago of a group of young

whites in Colorado who have a commune and are living by hunting deer. One man hunts for them. Some of the Indians gave him a chant or words to say. I haven't heard anything from the group now for three or four months but the last four times that he had gone out hunting deer this had happened: he goes alone, into the woods, into the mountains, stands there. He sees a group of deer. Three out of the last four times he has said the words that the Indians had taught him to say—one of the deer has detached itself from the group, walked into the clear and remained standing. The rest left. He shot that deer and took it home.

If all living things are in one net, could you use that same rationale to justify war, in that . . .

Go ahead, try it!

I don't want to, but it seems to me that that's one of the arguments that's used to justify war—the so-called just war—that by killing someone else you're preserving your own homeland or preserving a greater good.

I think there are some arguments that are very good for the just war. It happens that almost all of the wars that we participate in are unjust because they do not come from a natural defense of the community. Surely an ant has a right to defend itself from other ants who are attacking. But the problem with human wars is that evidently they come from undigested angers and aggressions inside "the ant heap." You know, it's an unintegrated being that we are. There's evidently some talk of that in a book called *Man into Ape*, I think it's by Lifton, who's a Jungian psychologist. His speculation is that human beings were originally herbivorous; maybe they came from another planet where they were quiet and gentle vegetarians. The conditions on this planet for climactic reasons got so that humans had to kill and eat animals to live. And human beings then learned ferocity from the animals that they were killing. Ferocity was unnatural to them—it is unintegrated in us, and we don't know what to do with it. And many vegetarians, and I'm sure you are one of them, Ghandi and others, are by eating vegetables actually trying to return to that situation, trying to go back and throw away this education in ferocity that was only half learned anyway. Sure, that's a marvelous thing to try to do. Anyway, that "poor education" throws an interesting light on the whole idea, doesn't it?

Kind of getting back to the idea of raising the consciousness of a college community, or St. Olaf in particular, how much value do you see in using energy for overt political protests or actions, and how much could be better directed toward inward spiritual growth? There's always a question of what should a person be doing?

Well, that's good! Gurdjieff said that we have an endless supply of energy. We have plenty of energy, both for outward things and inward things. But we don't spend it on either one. It's wasted. He described it as a leakage. We waste it by not really doing anything directly. We waste it, frittering it away in hundreds of tiny acts all the time, daydreaming. He said that at least half the energy available to us during the day is lost by daydreaming. Everytime you daydream you're picking up a memory, and the memory carries with it certain emotions, certain feelings. Every one of those emotions as it passes through your head draws on your supply of energy for that day. If you've ever noticed yourself in bed, daydreaming for an hour, you'll find you're exhausted after that hour. *education*

American life is lacking in concentration. The schools present you with seven to eight subjects every day. It's impossible for the child to develop any center. He can't tell the difference between triviality and intense expenditure of energy. This exhaustion can be seen clearly on the face of an American college student now, and it's getting worse. If you compare his look with the radiant look that you will see sometimes on the face of a young child, or on the face of a young African student, it's perfectly clear that energy is leaking out all over this American student. So it really isn't a choice between the two as it appears. If you can cut out the extraneous things, and stop the daydreaming, you would have plenty of energy both for inward and outward work. One hour of meditation a day is good and one demonstration every two weeks is plenty. Surely everybody's got enough energy for that.

Part of the problem is when students graduate into what is called the real world, many of the things that perhaps they would feel forced to do—to make a living—would be what could be considered trivial and not exactly contributing to their own spiritual progress.

So why kill yourself before you have to? But that's exactly right. More and more people are realizing this. Some people decide not to take jobs, because they don't want this leakage of energy all their lives. They don't want to have a heart attack when they're forty-five, and die of a sheer absence of energy. They decide to go into the communes; but the communes are having a lot of trouble because of the tremendous dissipation of energy that goes on inside them. The only communes that are really strong are communes like the Lama Foundation which are devoted to a lot of meditation every day. Merely not doing as your parents did is not sufficient. Instead of sitting around in office parties with energy drifting out, they sit daydreaming while they smoke grass or chat, and their energy goes in the same way. It's gone. By the end of the day they're exhausted and have accomplished nothing in growth.

Do you practice transcendental meditation or yoga to aid in your spiritual development.

I don't practice transcendental meditation, but I do sit every day. There are many kinds of meditation. Oh, maybe there's only one kind. I had some instruction from Tibetans in England; I'm not very much involved in Indian meditation, though I respect it. I'm also very interested in Christian meditation, which isn't much taught, but. . . .

Such as the Jesus prayer and Catholic chants?

Yes. I'm sure that the Eastern meditative awareness can be integrated into Christian stories, Christian figures, Christian psyche. But the Christian church is making no efforts in this direction at all, especially the Protestant church. I believe that it's going to be done anyway. Surely the interest in speaking in tongues and all of those things are evidence that so much of this unconscious material is taking place, whether the church wills it or no. . . .

On Unfinished Poets

An Interview with Scott Chisholm

Bemidji, Minnesota, July, 1969

In one of your essays for Choice, *you made this comment: "Poetry's purpose is to advance into an unknown country. This is why the question of audience is irrelevant. In order to penetrate into this country, poetry must learn to sleep differently, to awake differently, to listen for new sounds, to walk differently." Would you elaborate on this—keeping in mind your own work and your interest in Neruda and others?*

I think that a poem is a tiny model of the society in which it's born. The Elizabethan sonnet is a tiny model of the closed society and the class structure of the Elizabethans.

The contemporary poem attempts to be a model of the interior of the brain as well. The surrealist poem, for example, is a better model of human consciousness than the older linear poem because, as brain researchers now know, the mind evidently thinks in flashes and images. It does not think "logically" moving slowly from one point to the next. Thoughts appear in the mind as visual images, and at tremendous speed follow each other, somewhat like sudden flashes of filmscript. The modern film, therefore, is also an attempt to define—to reflect—the way human consciousness works.

The post-sonnet poem is like the film. Not only are we learning more about how the consciousness works, but we are also learning that the consciousness consists of flashes or images which change their content and mood very rapidly. Poetry is attempting now to catch up with the changes in the consciousness that have taken place over the last hundred years.

Our understanding of consciousness has probably changed more in the last hundred years than in any thousand year period before that. This is why the poem has changed more in the last hundred years than in the previous thousand. The narrative poem has disappeared. This doesn't mean that nobody can tell stories anymore, but it means that the narrative is not really useful now for describing what has been found out.

When I spoke of how poets have to learn to sleep differently, to awake differently, and to listen for new sounds, this is the sort of thing I had in mind. One of the ways we, as readers, become aware of the state of consciousness and the way it is changing is to read poetry. Since consciousness is changing with amazing speed, under the pressure of overpopulation as well as science as well as the kind of communication systems that McLuhan talks about, poetry finds itself with an opportunity to describe things that have never been described before—to throw out on the page the kinds of poem which has never been on the page before. And it is this excitement, in my opinion, that is drawing some of the poets forward. It's the possibility that if they're really sensitive to the inside of their skulls they'll be able to create a poem that will look different and actually *be* different than any poem written before.

the pressure of overpopulation

You once said that a poet must have "an awareness of the different kinds of fur a word has." I wonder if you would expand on that comment.

When I say *fur,* I mean all the unconscious associations that a word has. Some words have smells, like bodies, and as we know, the odor of a body carries a number of associations to the unconscious.

When the poet pays attention to the odor of words, his lines communicate instantly in a similar way. Before the reader has even grasped it conceptually, the *fur* of the words has communicated its world. The language has a sort of taproot.

You seem to have attempted to change the role of the poet in society by becoming more politically pugnacious.

Let's imagine the poem to be some kind of knife. The poet uses the poem to cut through the dead tissues in himself, and through certain filaments or sinews that are holding him to past patterns. He cuts away some of the cloudy stuff that holds him down.

But the poem can also be a two-edged knife, with two sharp edges. The whole thing moves like a pendulum and when the knife swings back, it swings away from the private and cuts into something public.

In Anglo-Saxon literary life we've always had the knife sharp on only one edge, with the other edge deliberately blunted, so that when it swung back into public life, it did not cut. The poet restricted his intensity so that it dealt only in private matters. The English, for example, deliberately blunt one side of the knife. It's perfectly clear that Pasternak, by contrast, uses a two-edged knife, whatever the tone of his political opinions, and when he wrote a poem or novel and it swung back, it cut. The

restricted his intensity

Russian writer-bureaucrats didn't like that. They didn't like the private edge being sharp and they didn't like the public edge being sharp.

In your early criticism in Choice *in which you state that poetry "must do something revolutionary both in language and in politics," are you describing the two edges of the knife?*

Yes.

But don't you see the United States with its political and social mutations as having something more immediate to occupy the would-be poet than a withdrawal into solitude? Or is it perhaps another type of solitude which you wish the poet to go into?

The poet doesn't need anything "immediate" to occupy himself with. He needs something deep to occupy himself with—and its unlikely at the start that that will be the political and social mutations of the United States. It's like some fairy tale in which he leaves a town and then he sees ahead of him the town getting closer and closer—the same town.

The Light Around the Body *strikes me as an outward book, a book against particular evils. Is there a contradiction, perhaps I'm wrong, between this book and your earlier critical position on "inward" poetry?*

There may be a contradiction. Just the same I think that every event has an inward and an outward reason for its happening. For example, if a man embezzles from a bank, the outward reason might be that he wants money;

the inward reason might be that he's looking for an excuse for suicide. After they're caught, some embezzlers feel the social humiliation to be a good reason to blow their brains out. So the inward reason for the embezzling was a desire to die. It had nothing to do with the money.

In the same way, an event like the Vietnam war can be traced to "imperialism" and financial manipulations. But the poems on the war in *The Light Around the Body* tried to give *inward* reasons for that war.

Who do you consider the major poets who will take the place of Eliot, Frost, and Pound?

Eliot, Frost, and Pound were odd writers in that they looked like statues, with a heavy and solid marble quality, while they were quite young. That is impressive.

Yet, at the same time, readers have not found them very helpful as spiritual guides. By contrast, the changes that have taken place in the poets of my generation have made them a kind of spiritual guide for many younger poets and readers. So no one will take the place of those three men. There won't be any immediate recurrence of the massive kind of poet. And that's all right.

Having just returned from an international poetry conference in England, how would you contrast the vitality of English and American poetry?

The English poets apparently feel themselves to be in the same static landscape where Eliot, Pound, and Auden found themselves thirty or forty years ago. They imagine that to write their poetry means to create a building into which they can invite a reader, whereas American poets think of writing poems as creating a living being, creating a horse, on which the reader can ride and get to some place he hasn't been.

Rightly or wrongly, we as readers imagine the older poets like Eliot and Pound to be pyramids—perhaps that is the optical illusion coming out of the universities. There poets are studied in *departments,* and, therefore, separated from the *flow* of time and they suddenly loom up at a fixed place on the horizon. And since the English have a greater susceptibility to university ideas than Americans, perhaps the pyramid mirage penetrates more deeply into them and makes their contemporary poets—except Ted Hughes and some younger poets like Pickard—more static and passive than American poets.

There is a considerable difference between audiences in England and America. The festival I attended had a London audience and it was perfectly clear that the audience had come to be entertained. The American poets, on the whole, were not there to entertain them, and the contrast was dramatic in the case of Robert Creeley whose readings always move me. He proceeds from word to word, not only with tremendous uncertainty, but also with a kind of anguish which is perfectly apparent in his voice and manner as he moves from one word to another. I remember thinking that his reading was, definitely, some form of nonentertainment. The English were baffled by his reading and didn't respond to it at all in the way an American audience would. They were baffled by my poems also. The English adored W. H. Auden and they adored Ogden Nash. These two poets were much in tune with the audience.

But in America in the last ten years—even more so during the last five years of the Vietnam war—you notice that the American audience is willing to be moved by poetry. They don't care so much about the entertainment. They laugh if you make jokes, but they're open to being *moved,* to feel some pain *with* you. So I've gained a new respect for the audiences in America—the audiences we do have.

Your generation has been called "the generation of 1962." Do you see any characteristics that group of poets has in common?

The generation includes Logan, Stafford, Jones, Ginsberg, and seven or eight others who come to mind. One thing they have in common is that they are all somewhat unfinished poets. They are open ended. By contrast, Eliot's first book was really a finished thing; Lowell's first book, elaborate and adult. Pound also began very early. But the poets of my generation, it seems to me, have a curious unfinished quality which is deep in them. Their first books were no good. They began very slowly. Like children putting blocks together, their first buildings were not castles, just huts. Poets like Eliot and Moore and Lowell somehow inherited a massive amount of usable ideas which acted as transformers to turn their psychic flow into literature. Wright, Stafford, Merwin, Hall, Kinnell, on the other hand, started slowly, and only by the age of thirty-five or forty did they begin to write well . . . the poets of the 1947 and 1917 generations had already written stunning books in their twenties. So it's a generation that's learned—a learning generation. It is still learning.

I think many of them also have a feeling—for the first time in American poetry—for specific *places* in the country. William Stafford has a powerful sense of Kansas and now the Oregon mountains. Snyder is rooted in Oregon—this binds him to Stafford in a curious way. How can you discuss James Wright without mentioning southern

Ohio? Yet when you think of Ciardi, Nims, Jarrell, Schwartz, you never think of a state, let alone a part of the state. Lowell had a great feeling for Boston, but it was more for New England culture, than for a piece of the ground.

Also I notice a wonderful sense of companionship and comradeship in the generation. Poets as distinct as Creeley and Hall, or Ginsberg and Kinnell have a sense of something they want to accomplish together and have a desire to help each other in any way they can. At least this has been my experience.

The First Ten Issues of *Kayak*

An Essay

I

George Hitchcock asked me for some prose for *kayak,* and I asked if I might do an attack on his first ten issues. He thought that was a good idea.

Some people feel that criticism is always destructive, like an overexposure to X-rays. That fear comes from concentration on criticism a decade ago. Those in the Lowell-Shapiro generation were not good critics. They were always looking up into the sky: who was there? Yeats. His blazing rocket arching across the sky. His solitary rocketlike career was the only model they accepted for their own lives. They acted as if every writer was for himself. Each poet had his own rocket launching pad, separate from the others. It was important to keep the formula for your rocket fuel secret, otherwise the others might catch you! Your obligation to the other rockets was to throw off their timing. (Norman Mailer's gossipy sneers at his novelist friends is a good example of this.) The poet's criticism was either sheer gush (out of ignorance or guilt) or a transparent attempt to weaken competitors.

Partly out of reaction to this sterile and mutual hostility, the Black Mountain poets in the early fifties made loyalty into a heroic virtue. They still refuse to make judgments of anyone if he has professed loyalty to the Olson creed. Whatever their doubts in private, in public not a word of criticism falls from their lips. (Creeley's reviews in *Poetry* are examples of this.) They save all their hostility for outsiders. (Prose in the Grove Press anthology is an example of that.) But reviews by fine poets that keep mum on important flaws of their contemporaries confuse younger poets, who end up distrusting their own critical instincts.

These two approaches to criticism, capitalistic dog-eat-dog competitiveness and corporative "don't knock the company" team-spirit, both seemed good ideas at the time, but both approaches now seem big failures. There is a third possibility: those who are interested in the same sort of poetry attack each other sharply, and still have respect and affection for each other. I don't see why this approach should be impossible for Americans. Criticism does not imply contempt. The criticism of my own poetry that has been the most use to me has been criticism that, when I first heard it, utterly dismayed me.

Turning to *kayak* then, I think the first ten issues have been on the whole clogged and bad. As an editor, George Hitchcock is too permissive. Poets are encouraged to continue in their failures as well as their fresh steps. Sometimes I think George is more interested in printing four issues a year—he loves to see those wild looking pages go through!—than what is *in* the issues. Like the Provencal lover, he goes through incredible pains, but it's possible he is in love with the idea of having a magazine, as the Provencal poets were said to be in love with the idea of being in love.

Too much foggy stuff gets in: in *kayak* poems usually someone is stepping into a tunnel of dark wind and disappearing into a whistle; the darkness is always pausing to wait for someone. One gets the feeling that as long as there are a few skeletons of fossil plants in the poem, or some horses floating in the mind, or a flea whispering in Norwegian, in it goes!

The images even take on a certain grammatical skeleton of their own. For instance they are made of *a*) an animal or object, *b*) a violent action, *c*) an adjective (often *tiny, dark,* or *great*), and then *d*) the geographical location. "Lighted cigars fall like meteors on a deserted football field in Pierre, South Dakota" (no. 3, p. 17); "Birds fly in the broken windows / of the hotel in Argyle" (no. 3, p. 32); "Black beetles, bright as Cadillacs, toil down / The long dusty road into the mountains of South Dakota" (no. 5, p. 31). Sometimes the place comes first: "In Wyoming a horse dies by a silver river" (no. 1, p. 7).

There get to be a lot of passives: "Policemen were discovered in the cupolas waving felt erasers" (no. 7, p. 37); and partial passives: "Hands are choking a cat in a small liquor store in Connecticut" (no. 1, p. 7).

Often, to end the poem, an image with literary resonance will be followed instantly with an off-hand remark from the world of truck-drivers. "I pick two apples, / then leave the cold park. / That's all I can do." "Another beer truck comes to town, / chased by a dog on three legs. // Batman lies drunk in the weeds." (no. 3, p. 32). "At the farther / End of the mind, a farmer / Douses the lamp and climbs / The narrow stairs to sleep. // All night, under the window, / A horse gallops in the pasture." (no. 5, p. 42).

Moreover, all *kayak* poems seem to take place in the eternal present: the poet uses the present progressive tense—past and future tenses have died out. As a result, those hands are still choking that poor cat in the liquor store, and the horse is forever galloping up and down in that pasture.

At the same time *kayak* is valuable, and a much-loved magazine. Unlike the *Kenyon Review,* which everyone for years has been hoping would kick off soon, *kayak* would be missed very much if it developed a leak and sank. George offers some kind of nourishment. Every hand of course is sometimes open, sometimes closed. As a fist, *kayak* is raised against stuff like this; crystallized flower formations from the jolly intellectual dandies:

> Mind in its purest play is like some bat
> That beats about in caverns all alone,
> Contriving by a kind of senseless wit
> Not to conclude against a wall of stone.
>
> Wilbur

But *kayak* is also against the high-pitched batlike cry of the anal Puritan mandarin:

> That I cannot take
> and that she will not
>
> not give, but will not
> have it taken.
>
> Sorrentino

This trapped, small-boned, apologetic, feverish, glassy, intellectualist fluttering is just what George hates. He has tried to provide a place where poems that escape from that glass box can come. If you turn into a fish, he has a muddy pond, with lots of foliage.

Then too, the dark wells and wet branches and drunks-sleeping-happily-in-cellars images that we see so often in *kayak* say important things in themselves: they are hints to the mind that it can escape if it wants to. Of course adoption of a style cannot make a poet free. The mind has too many tricks in reserve for that—it hates change. In order to keep a restless poet quiet, the rational mind will even slide down to him some floating breast images and extinct dinosaur bone images, perhaps enough for a whole poem! But these images can remain perfectly rational. When we read them, we feel something not genuine there. Poems of that sort are like movies of mountain scenery shown on the inside of a stationary train window.

So a lot of poems that *appear* to have escaped from the mind-walls really haven't escaped at all. A conventional form of the underground lakes poem is beginning to appear, and *kayak* publishes too many of them. Of course that is not all George's fault: he is publishing the best poems he can get, and he has published some marvelous ones, about fifty at least. In fact, some of the best poems he has published have nothing to do with what I have called here "the *kayak* poem": for example, the wonderful poems by William Lane, "Green" in no. 4, "Turning" and "What to Do Till the Answer Comes" in no. 10; Jean Batie's poem "I Saw My Mother on the Stair" in no. 9; David Ignatow's bagel poem in no. 7 and "Political Cartoon" in no. 10; John Ridland's "Yachting Scene" and "Sunkist Packing Plant" in no. 5; William Pillin's frightening poem "Look Down!" in no. 3; Richard Hugo's "Castel Sant'Angelo" in no. 2; Bert Meyers's "A Tree Stump at Noon" and "They Who Waste Me" in no. 5; Louis Simpson's "Progress" in no. 5; and John Woods's "Some Martial Thoughts" in no. 10. The truth is we don't write enough good poems to fill a large magazine like *kayak*.

II

Turning to the poets then, if a poet has written a conventional *kayak* poem, what mistake has he made? First of all, I think he has mistaken a way of living for a style.

Looking through *kayak,* one sees many poems on trees, leaves, animals, plants, nature poems. But it is clear from reading them that the poet at the moment he wrote them was not really out in the field, he was not alone out there in the nonhuman; on the contrary, he was sitting at his desk, in his usual place. (The poems of John Haines are exceptions to this.)

Many *kayak* poets, turning away from the rhetorical verse of the Fugitives or the hairy wits, have aimed at a greater simplicity of style. But simplicity is a natural expression of solitude, just as cluttered complexity and rhetorical flourish are the natural expression of an oversocialized life, a life with too many people in it. So the next step for many poets who want to write better is not to learn more about the style, but to stop their usual sociability. That step is difficult for many American poets who are teaching in universities, where sociability is forced upon them by the nature of their work. Poets in artistic colonies or hippie colonies are better off, but still are within a sociable world. Almost all American poets insist on their right to be sociable.

Basho said, "To express the flavor of the inner mind, you must agonize during many days." That is a wonderful sentence! The purpose of it all is not to write long endless poems, but to express "the flavor of the inner mind." That phrase suggests how alive the senses must be to do that, and also suggests that we step into that mind through pain. Basho thought the poet should be willing to live in solitude, which is occasionally painful and lonely. In one of his best poems, Basho makes clear that the true poem is not associated with what Freud calls the "pleasure principle" (sociability, eating, consuming), but rather with the "pain principle":

pleasure principle
pain principle

Dried salmon
And Kuya's breakthrough into the spirit,
Both in the cold time of the year!

(Kuya was a young monk of an earlier time who one day in December suddenly made the Zen "leap," and spent the rest of his life helping the poor.)
The Japanese say, Go to the pine if you want to learn about the pine. If an American poet wants to write of a chill and foggy field, he has to stay out there, and get cold and wet himself. Two hours of solitude seem about right for every line of poetry.

窮人協樂部

poor people association

協助貧困 Sherry 맣이 이용

11.25. 1999
같이 starbucks

poor people Club

165

7-8

Three Poems

Looking Out to Sea

It is Biddeford Pool, Maine. Rags of snow still lie on the hairy earth north of us. The old split-brained rocks point up out of the bay. These Silurian boulders have been looked at by so many Boston women, so many husbands desperately relaxing by an alien sea, kids screaming in both ears, but they have not become mirror people anyway. They look up at the sky, satisfied with the constellations as they are, lazily whirling about in the serious black sky.

Two sealheads appear not far out . . . they resemble off-shaped balloons . . . so sleek, whiskered, so cold and alone in the aloneness. Farther out a flock of ten or twelve, smaller heads, bobbing, a ship's mast in the background.

This is their morning, it is a good morning, a morning that takes its place in the series of vertical scratches made on an old board, made on the pole of the constellation, a morning that follows a night, a night when a man has slept with a woman.

In a Boat on Big Stone Lake

1

How beautiful it is, aging, to be out with friends
on the water! Already, in June,
the water heavy with green filaments
of life. Spring birds send in a warning
from the South Dakota shore.

2

The briefness of life! How the yellow rope
shines in the water-walking sun!
From inside us, deep ages
walk across the water, buildings
fall, the angel has spread its wings
over the dark valley of tiny minutes.

3

The country staggers toward light-
hearted brutality.
We have made a long journey
and no one knows who is coming back.
I remember the muskrat's head so sleek.
I remember something floating on the water.

Looking into Eyes

I look into your eyes, and am drawn suddenly into the deepest chambers of the Pharoah's warehouses, where the stars are kept in grain bags. It is the center of a pool, beneath it fires pull me, into deepest fires where the dark brown wood smoulders for centuries under the water near the bowl and the keys made of hair. It is a badger of God in the mountains, a lioness lying in an onyx bowl, the night sky above the blue sands, and the lamb by the stone wall, and snow on the hillside, boats on the sea.

IV

An Argument about the Meaning of the Word "Craft"

Craft Interview

With Mary Jane Fortunato and Cornelia P. Draves,
and with Paul Zweig and Saul Galin

Spring, 1972

So what are we going to talk about?

Craft.

That covers many sins. These friends, Saul Galin and
Paul Zweig, are here, and I'd like them to join the con-
versation whenever they feel like it, if that's all right
with you.

When did you start writing poetry?

In 1962 I published my first book. I started writing in
1946 or 1947, so I had been writing for fifteen or sixteen
years before I published *Silence in the Snowy Fields* in
1962.

You are still living up to your reputation of personally
answering all submissions promptly, sometimes with a
note making astringent but helpful comments. And are
not these comments generally geared to the craft of the
poem?

I do still try to write notes on every submission I get. But I don't think they're related to the craft of the poem in most cases. In many cases I might say something like "I don't feel you have really touched on anything really important to your life," which can't be "craft." Yet it seems to me this is what's wrong with most poems I see.

And you have said that you consider Latin American poetry the best poetry being written today. Do you mean because its imagery is well crafted?

No. It's very difficult to understand craft in another language. And what drew me to Neruda . . . I was drawn to him before I knew anything of his craft. It's the depth and passion, passion and depth of feeling, I suppose.

You are not only a champion of the Latin American poetry but you have also translated a good deal of it. Do you think this has influenced your own approach to the image?

Oh, I'm sure it has.

Pablo Neruda says that of the thirty languages into which his poetry has been translated, it translates best into the Italian because of the similarity between the two languages. He finds the English language so different from the Spanish, so much more direct that sometimes in the translation only the meaning and not the atmosphere of the poetry comes through. Is this true?

I can't positively say. I don't know the Italian translations. Anyway, it's not due to craft.

Paul Zweig: Well, it could have to do with craft in the

sense of the skills it takes to put words together. The texture of words.

True, but then we get involved in whether Neruda's English translations have been good or bad. Because if a translation only gives "the meaning and not the atmosphere" it could be the fault of the English language or of the translator.

P. Z.: Exactly. Then the question is, is it possible to make a good translation in English?

Yes. And I think Neruda's wrong.

You have written about the conflict you feel exists between the technique and what you call the "imaginative association." Would you want to enlarge or comment on that statement?

No. I wrote an essay called "Looking for Dragon Smoke" in which I tried to drag myself through that marsh, and I oversimplified, but I said that basically a poet has the choice to try to spend his time working on technique, which has been the typical American habit, or he could spend his time trying to deepen his associational links which seems to be the South American and European way.

Would you say that the technique of Ginsberg was to put emphasis on improvisation?

You can't make a statement, I think, about the *technique of Ginsberg*. In other words, the number of things that Ginsberg does could not be summed up under one word "technique."

Do you differentiate between technique and craft?

Hmmm.

P. Z.: Well, I suppose a person could make a comparison between technique as applied to poetry and technique as it applies to what a shaman does. A shaman has all kinds of techniques to get himself into ecstasy and to excite other people.

You want me to answer these questions? I have some confused thoughts. I dislike the word "craft," when we talk of poetry. "Craft" suggests an inanimate object, as when we say a carpenter crafts a chest of drawers. But somebody's already made the wood. So therefore, thinking of it, I would rather . . . my idea is this: perhaps making the poem from the beginning involves three separate areas of experience. The first experience . . . is interior. When the poet realizes for the first time . . . when he touches for the first time, something far inside of him. It's connected with what the ancients called The Mysteries, and it's wrong to talk of it very much. Some poets have the experience very early. Wordsworth said that he had experienced it when he was seven or eight years old. And others when they're fifteen, sixteen, seventeen. Whitman, interestingly enough, did not have this experience until he was about thirty-seven years old. Before that, he was writing merely well-crafted newspaper verse. Then, when he touched another center inside—or when he—or you can use the metaphor of finding a well if you want—or you could talk of it as breaking through an ego wall but I don't think it's as useful—if any person comes near that experience he or she will never forget it the rest of his life. If he writes poetry it will come from that.

You can talk of that as an *experience*. We could call

cunning

this stage wholly interior. Then there's a second necessary stage which I don't see described very much, but which I would call something like cunning. And cunning involves the person's rearranging his life in such a way that he can feel the first experience again. This is worldly, and involves common sense. The word cunning appears in Joyce. In "silence, exile and cunning." And the cunning in Whitman—evidently he felt the experience often when he was with human beings! . . . Unlike Wordsworth . . . so the cunning in Whitman was to spend a lot of time riding the street cars, jostling human beings, crossing on the Brooklyn Ferry, etc. For Rilke, who was temperamentally exactly the opposite of Whitman—though the initial experience has a similar resonance—cunning meant finding long periods of solitude. Inside the city or outside the city. And he had such faith in the water he had found! He felt marriage was impossible for him, since he could not have . . . evidently the solitude he needed was so deep and so long that he willingly endured years of loneliness. He endured about ten years of loneliness again late in his life without writing a word, always hopeful that the poems would come; and, eventually, when he was able to live for a few weeks in a tower on the shore of the Adriatic he wrote the *Sonnets* and the *Duino Elegies* . . . if he hadn't had that second worldly cunning, you would have had one book from Rilke perhaps and no more. Few American writers seem to understand this cunning. We've had lots of brilliant novelists, too, like Glenway Wescott who wrote one great novel and never wrote another one.

Then, you have something which could be called—I don't exactly know what to call it—but the third stage—forgive this scheme—could be called something like "letting the animal live." I prefer something like that to the idea of craft, because what is involved is psychic energy.

He had such faith in the water he had found

175

We have a mixed metaphor if we imagine living energy as a chest of drawers. Living energy is more growing the tree than shaping the tree . . . and then . . . I've lost it again now. . . . But you never say that nature *crafts* a tree. And yet we know we have to have wood in order to get furniture. So we've got to go back beyond craft if we're going to talk about it.

P. Z.: What you're saying really—of the three stages, the first can't be learned in the ordinary sense.

Yes, that's good.

P. Z.: The second can be learned in a sense, in a general sense, the way you say someone learns how to live. You can probably be taught the third. You can't be taught the first; you can be taught the second a little; you can be taught the third probably quite a lot.

Once you're into the first and second you can be helped in the area of the third. For example, well, using clichés in trying to express an incredible thought.

Well, the danger of talking of craft in the *New York Quarterly* and the danger of craft-talk as it appears in the writing workshops is . . . the staggering thing in the United States is that the emphasis on technique and craft comes too early, before the wood has actually been grown. Before either of the first two stages have been passed through. Most teachers don't even talk about it— they *assume* the student has passed through the first two stages and what he needs is craft—the assumption is wrong. . . .

P. Z.: Even beyond what we've talked about—you know craft can be learned and learned very proficiently by someone seventeen or eighteen years old, before he has reached the age of pain.

Mmmm. That's interesting. The hope then is that that poet will become dissatisfied with his own talent and he will notice there is a difference between his work and the work of Rilke. Suppose that the head of his workshop is able to get some of his students' well-crafted poems into the *New Yorker*—and the poet then becomes successful in his twenties; the danger is that he will never go back and try to experience the first and second stage. He'll stumble on and the critics will not be able to tell the difference anyway.

But the first and second stages have to be perfected through the third stage.

What does that mean—perfected?

You have to insert skill, do you not?

I don't know. Lawrence was a novelist. He doesn't seem to be taken seriously as a poet. He is without "skill" and yet when his poems come out, one out of fifteen or one out of twenty of them is marvelous. If a man has experienced certain things, I'm not sure how much craft is essential in order to do something that's really . . . marvelous . . . that really has psychic energy. The most important thing is psychic energy. If the craft kills that, obviously we're worse off than we were before. But I know what you're hinting at, so keep on with the question.

You object to teaching craft in a workshop. I agree that the poet has not reached the age of pain. But one can hardly say, "Tell me how much pain you have had be-

fore I let you into my class." Is he going to sit around talking about how many days he cried or something like that?

The age of pain—I don't know what is meant by the age of pain—I'm not sure pain is the point here—but what it suggests to me is a situation in which the student feels the particular pain of being absolutely, finally up against the wall . . . and where is he going to turn? But if he crafts his poem well, most of the teachers in our workshops will not allow him that pain. They will praise it, and then that pain will go away. I don't mean crying, but the other . . .

P. Z.: So many experts in line endings . . .

Someone told me a wonderful story about the Iowa workshop. A mood of anxiety had settled over the place—it was a few years ago. And one man set himself to trace the source of it, which he found to be a poet who was in the habit of saying that publishing a poem in *Poetry* was like being a colonel—if you publish in a mimeographed magazine you're a private—you see—and publishing in a magazine like *Prairie Schooner* is being a lieutenant . . . but publishing a poem in the *New Yorker* was like being a *general*. . . .

The categorization—you're stamped.

And how American it is! The military metaphor is there. . . .

But in workshops you always have this pendulum swing. You can always get into the area of value judgments.

How strong was that image? How much does it affect me? That's the opposite. That's the alternative.

P. Z.: The danger in that sort of talk is that the teacher gets in the position of making moral *judgments.*

Well, I think of one of the ways that John Logan teaches. I think he's one of the best teachers of poetry in the United States, maybe in the West. I've seen him once or twice in a workshop and a student comes in with one of his poems which may be well crafted or maybe not and he doesn't make any value judgments. He brings in one of his own poems with his own grief in it, and he begins to talk about the poem, his own loneliness, his own grief, and his own sorrow, and the student suddenly realizes that this is John Logan with the very feeling that he has written about, and nothing is said, and the student just goes home and throws away the poem, or looks at it and . . . you understand me? That is a marvelous way to teach.

Perhaps other workshop teachers are not up to John Logan.

It doesn't matter—it doesn't matter. It means that there's depth of feeling here. And evidently Theodore Roethke used to teach the same way. He taught Jim Wright this way. Not teaching craft so much as—well—what we've talked about.

What about your own cunning? What about your life? What do you think your cunning involves?

My cunning involved going out to the Middle West and

into a farm place where I didn't have to earn much money and where I could be alone for long periods of time.

Well, let's go on to imagery. Your poetry is characterized by the use of imagery. To quite a great extent.

Let's imagine a poem as if it were an animal. When animals run, they have considerable flowing rhythms. Also they have bodies. An image is simply a body where psychic energy is free to move around. Psychic energy can't move well in a non-image statement—think up one. . . .

Saul Galin: The sweetness of the apple?

No, don't bring any senses in. "The politician must have a clear mental grasp of his constituency." Now it has no imagery to speak of, and there's no living psychic energy moving through it. An image is not anything unusual. It is simply language used in such a way that the psychic energy can continue its flow. It's our *minds* that are categorized and talk of imagery as if it were a dead thing. A poet says, "Well, I'd like to have some images in my poem." That sounds as if he were saying, "I think I'll go out and pick up some (dead) rocks on the beach."

P. Z.: Freud said something that really struck me—dreams are fantastic in that dreams are not just images—they talk—they are full of meaning just as language is full of meaning. Dreams take your emotions—the things you see—the words you say—all the fifty different sources of life impressions—and translate them into this kind of discord which is visual.

I like that idea. I suggested that we were letting an animal live, but it's perfectly clear to everyone, including the poet and those who are reading it, that the poem is also conveying . . . conveying something—that once he has created the poem, the poem gives a message to the poet himself. The message can be a message about his own spiritual life. If you remember, in Theodore Roethke's last book, there was a poem which had an image that he had saved in notebooks for years—"the paralytic in the tub, the water rising." Finally a few months before he died it found its way into a poem. It was a prediction of what would happen to him. He drowned in the "rising water," in the swimming pool. So there are messages, as in dreams, embedded in poems. So that, following Paul, you'd have to imagine the poem as a living creature who talks to you. And the problem is understanding what the poem means, what the images say. The poet understands them moderately or half understands them. The audience half understands them. Is that a matter of craft? Chests of drawers don't talk.

If we're talking about images from a craft viewpoint, what would you say are the requirements of a good image? For instance, these lines from Blake "how the chimney-sweepers cry / every black'ning Church appalls!"

Yes. All right. As we know, Blake's images have a staggering power. I'll make two suggestions. One is that a strong image, as opposed to a good image, contains several of the senses in it, not only one. Now that one that you said: "the black'ning. . . ." What was that again?

"how the chimney-sweepers cry / every black'ning Church appalls!"

It has a sound that involves a color. He has other lines in that same poem: "how the hapless soldier's sigh / runs in blood down Palace walls." That's wild. All you have to do is to say: "how the Vietnam soldier's sigh / runs in blood down the White House walls." You have then an anguish—which is turned into a liquid—no—there is a sound which is turned into a liquid and which is now running red down a white wall. And you can taste it—feel it—and see it. Here is a poem by Basho:

> The temple bell stops
> but the sound keeps coming
> out of the flowers.

It's hard for us as Westerners to be sensitive even to one or two of the senses at the same time. Here he is not only sensitive to two: he has changed the sound into an odor. Another poem of his goes this way:

> The sea grows dark.
> The voices of the wild ducks
> turn white.

The strong image has an intermingling of several senses. The abstract statement has no senses in it at all. "Individuality is decreasing in our culture." Nothing. Nothing. Nothing. In many poems I read there's not one thing that you can see or feel. Their senses have been numbed by living inside the four walls of a school.

In images like those in Blake's poems there will also be an intermingling of *worlds*. He gives us a mother-pity world. . . . He talks of this quite a lot. And then he suddenly drives across that with a political fact—"the hapless soldier's sigh," or the Church being blackened by the Industrial Revolution. That's a different world. So he will take the world of compassion, then he'll cross it with a political reality like the Industrial Revolution, then he'll cross it again with spiritual life, which is a separate and third thing. Then he may take the opinions of Newton—what's wrong with science—he may cross it a fourth time and suddenly they're all inside.

We know in everyday life that these worlds cross here—rmmm, rmmm—without warning anyone.

What about some of your own images? "The Teeth Mother Naked at Last"—you say the "scream lashes like a tail" and "the whines of jets pierce like long needles"— you have the tactile, sight, and sound. They're all in there.

Obviously I've been reading Blake.

Well, you know Stephen Stepanchev says that sometimes surrealist-derived technique gets in the way of your themes.

That's a ghastly statement.

That's a quote.

I know that. You know I'm not getting after Stepanchev, but—read that sentence to me again.

Sometimes your "surrealist-derived technique gets in the way of your themes," and he was referring particularly to some of your poems in The Light Around the Body.

There may be bad poems there, I'm used to that possibility. What struck me about his statement was the language. The sentence implies that the images and the themes come from two different sources. It also implies that unless one surrealist had written in that "technique" none of the rest could have. But where did the first surrealist get it then? So the word surrealist-derived is very strange. Then allowing the senses into a poem is described as a technique. That is precisely what it isn't. It's an old book, and he may have changed his mind, but . . .

Well, although most of your images, is this true, are subjective, you do use some of the so-called images from reality?

I won't accept either the word "subjective" that Stephen Stepanchev and others have used or "the deep image" or the idea that subjective images are somehow opposed to reality.

Well, do you think that a poet should familiarize himself with numerous rhetorical devices such as oxymoron, anastrophe, synecdoche, and so forth in order to perfect the craft of his poetry?

Read that sentence again.

Do you think that a poet should familiarize himself with numerous rhetorical devices such as oxymoron, anastrophe, synecdoche, and so forth in order to perfect the craft of his poetry?

All those words are horribly boring when you read them to me. The sound of them—they're all Greekish. Isn't it odd that we haven't developed Anglo-Saxon words? Words with senses in them that would describe these things? Do you follow me? We're not satisfied with the Greek word for pig for example. We get our own word for pig. We have our own word for house. We think houses are important. It's odd that these words you mention exist only in Greek form. I don't think that to us, even to you, they are very important.

I think you will find many of those devices used in modern poetry and they enhance the poetry.

But remember what T. S. Eliot said: "Well, you know I have never been able to remember the difference between anapestic and trochaic."

He doesn't have to remember that.

If he doesn't have to remember, who does then?

That's a little bit different.

How? How is it different?

P. Z.: You have pointed out something very important. These words have a real use. They help in trying to figure out, later, your experience with a poem. So they are helpful retrospectively.

Right. But the language is too alien to the poem. Imagine a naturalist studying, for example, a partridge. And it's important for him in distinguishing between two kinds of partridges to say that one has a reticulated comb. But the partridge doesn't think he has a reticulated comb. He thinks it's terrific.

P. Z.: The whole tendency of Robert's answers is to make the word "craft" seem inappropriate.

Your friend defined techniques before as something,

for example, a shaman might do to get himself into the mood to do what he has to do.

Mmmm.

Do you object to questions about techniques?

What the shaman experiences as rituals is what I would call cunning.

What do you consider to be the most common faults of a poorly crafted poem? If you would look at a poem, and view it purely from a craft viewpoint—

I wouldn't do that. I'd refuse to do that.

You can't imagine doing that in a craft interview?

No, I wouldn't do that. Not even for the sake of a craft interview.

Before we get too far away from this cunning thing—the cunning and the technique—I'd like to ask a few questions about writing to music and so forth. Could we do that here? What about something like carrying a fragment around for a long time? Or a line that just isn't working yet.

I keep some of them in my head and I have an entire folder at home of which the title is "Fragments."

That's what I wanted to ask at the beginning.

I do keep notebooks, but I keep tons of these failed poems. Some of them I keep because there was one moment of flow in them. The rest of the poem was just put in by the ego or some stiff part of the mind.

Do you write when the image happens? Do you stop whatever you are doing?

I remember a poem in *Silence in the Snowy Fields* when I was . . . when I saw a wooden board lying there in front of my chicken house and it was sort of half wet. The snow was melting. And there were tracks of chickens around it. And I lifted it up to see if there were tracks of chickens underneath and there were! Somebody had thrown the board down there. Anyway that—suddenly I had a longing for a poem. So therefore for me it's lucky to have old boards hanging around.

Do you advise poets to listen to the American speech rhythms? Deliberately listen to them?

The poet may as well. He hasn't got anything else to do.

P. Z.: Isn't it possible though that listening to speech rhythms and modeling your poems on speech rhythms can become a mannerism?

What is this about listening to Americans? I mean, we are Americans. So all you have to do is listen to yourself.

But you have to do it consciously.

Yes, I guess so. Consciously. We do have to listen to it consciously because consciously an old literary rhythm has already been given us in high school.

P. Z.: There's something in the language of The Light

When a sentence is alive

Around the Body *which I thought involved a big difference from* Silence in the Snowy Fields. *It seems that instead of moving along in colloquial speech rhythms in* The Light *there's a kind of high language that you restore. And I think this is magnificent. I can think of about a dozen poems in the book with a high language—old language—but it's not fighting the fight of speech language against . . .*

There's a possibility of taking in language that comes from other worlds, and then keeping this sense of ordinary speech rhythms, and trying to let the language build up like a wave on top of an ocean swell.

That's a matter of craft.

At the same time what guides this craft is an instinctive animal sense for when a sentence is alive and when it is not alive. For example, William Carlos Williams: "This is just to say that I have eaten the plums that were in the icebox."

Yes.

So, suppose instead of saying "This is just to say" he had written down: "One thing I would like to remark on is that I have eaten the plums." As Frost would say, that sentence now has no "sentence sound." Frost's letter about that is magnificent—it's in James Scully's book, *Modern Poetics.*

*As far as your edition—*Forty Poems Touching on Recent American History—*what determined the selection of the poems you included in that edition? You said you se-*

lected them because they had an imaginative force as giving a picture of the United States. But what I wanted to ask is, did you look at them from their craft viewpoint?

Not in the slightest.

Not in the slightest. But you did say that the political poem needed an especially fragrant language.

Yes.

I should say the selection of poems for an edition or an anthology would be viewed by a great many poets from a craft point of view. And I don't think that's bad.

No. No. But it's so hard to find good poems about American history that you have a lot of things to worry about besides that.

Then you have this collection of tiny poems—The Sea and the Honeycomb: A Book of Tiny Poems. Now, why and how the tiny poems? Do you think there's a difference in craft as applied to the tiny poem?

Again "craft applied to." The poet who is writing a tiny poem that is good is basically refusing to talk, refusing to allow the flow to come out until it has shaped itself into some explosive and brief form. Then as soon as it comes out he falls silent. So I really don't think you can consider that as a matter of craft.

Is it a matter of technique though? I think technique and craft have a differentiation in their meanings.

P. Z.: You have an essay, don't you, about short poems?

And you say something that has always stuck in my mind—that there are certain types of experience which are by their nature very brief and if one is to talk about these brief experiences, one has to develop a kind of language that is willing to deal with them—to imitate in language what happens in experience. To use language in a brief way.

You have in America ten thousand haikus written every year but all of them are crafted. They take the typical rambling of English poetical language and chop it off. But evidently the haiku represents a totally different experience—I've lost it now—

Well, we don't agree with you that all the haiku written in English are not good.

I've never seen a haiku written in the English language. I don't believe there is one. I have yet to see one.

Have you read American Haiku Magazine? *Do you think none of them are haiku?*

None of them. I read the magazine very carefully because I was going to write an essay for them. The Japanese say the haiku is a poem in which there's a tiny explosion inside—and if that's not there—I don't care how many syllables it's got—then it's not a haiku. And that little tiny explosion brings the life to this creature.

P. Z.: It seems to me the Zen point of view is that if anyone has the nature of experience revealed to him through his own discipline, he sees all the experiences of life as a series of explosions. A flower opening is the way everything happens. There is no plot in history at all.

Blyth's four volumes on haiku are wonderful. He often mentions Thoreau in those books. One day Thoreau is sitting by his door and it's raining. And he said something like: "This raindrop and I draw close to each other". He wrote it as prose but Blyth implies it may be a genuine haiku.

P. Z.: Of course we were talking before not only about haiku, but also about short poems.

Yes.

Didn't you have some haiku in your anthology?

I had a few—out of seventy short poems I included in Beacon's new edition of *The Sea and the Honeycomb*, I think about sixteen are haiku.

How do you think the contemporary long poem differs from the traditional long poem? That's a matter of technique.

That's a good question. I'll just repeat what I've heard now. And that is, that for reasons no one understands the narrative line which was useful in the old poem is no longer useful. Browning wouldn't admit this, and he kept trying. Eliot suspected the failure of Browning and he and Pound both tried the narrative line in a drawing room situation—"Portrait of a Lady." But when Eliot got around to write his own long poem he understood the curious fact very well, that somehow the narrative line was finished. And so in the *Wasteland* he deliberately breaks the narrative line—keeps moving the parts around—I haven't thought about the reason why the narrative line has failed but I accept the idea. It seems to me really—it has something to do with the Industrial Revolution. I called an earlier poem "After the Industrial Revolution Everything Happens at Once." The man down in Missouri who did the long Indian epics—Neihardt—the same man who interviewed Black Elk—believed in craft in the traditional way. And he insisted that there were no new issues in craft. He wrote in the old iambic line and he rhymed and he used the old narrative line. He crafted them very well. But the long poems are not very alive.

What about Roethke's sequences?

I like them. It's as if to write a long poem today you have to be tremendously at home inside your mind. Because the sequences are taking place somehow inside the mind.

P. Z.: Is there a successful long poem? I'm thinking of Galway. And that's certainly a successful book, although he claims it's a single long poem.

I don't think it's a long poem at all.

You're talking about The Book of Nightmares?

The Book of Nightmares. Yes, it's ten poems.

What about Whitman's long poems? Are they broken up?

Yes, into sequences—small sequences too. Of course it's perfectly possible that there's a way to write a poem which we are too clumsy and sluggish to understand.

P. Z.: Other people are trying to write long poems.

Yes, Duncan's long poems are very impressive. What I'm really saying is that since the narrative has failed there may be another way to write which we literally haven't found.

You have written quite a few prose poems. What is gained by a prose poem?

Nothing is gained, it's just interesting. In a prose poem you can bring in all sorts of details. All sorts. In *Paradise Lost* for example, fingernails are rarely mentioned—belt buckles are never mentioned, hummm? Little strings of hair—soup is never mentioned. Ear lobes are not mentioned. All of these fantastic details. . . . In the rolling rhythms of a poem, it is difficult to put in these "insignificant details." Chinese poetry, by the way, seems to be low key all the way through like our prose poems . . . Whitman and Robinson Jeffers and Milton love the roll of the ocean. But a prose poem is more like a lake. The Chinese poets are interested in quiet lake poems with a transparency you can see down into.

P. Z.: What about experiments in prose poetry?

We need to calm the language down.

In your prose poem about the caterpillar you have detail after detail. And I think that's true of all prose poems of yours that we've read. They all end with a twist, a different tone, at the end.

Hmmmmm.

It surprised us.

Did it? I don't want to bore you at the end.

Would you like to tell us what gives birth to an idea for a poem?

No.

Okay. Now this is purely craft. You have said that rhyme in the English language has been exhausted.

Yes.

There's a question mark after that.

Oh, really? I just thought it was a simple statement that every one agreed to. Really rhyme is connected with singing poems. When a human being has stopped singing poems, there's no purpose in end rhyming. I don't want to get after rhyme too much; but it seems to me an unnatural baroque embellishment. X. J. Kennedy wants very much—you know he has a new magazine *Countermeasure* in which he talks a great deal about craft—I'm glad to see this magazine—you need to have these things explored, but it's a little too much like workshops.

But you do use off rhyme in your poems to a considerable degree. You take these last three lines of "Watching Television" which are: "The filaments of the soul slowly separate / The spirit breaks, a puff of dust floats up / Like a house in Nebraska that suddenly explodes." And you use assonance there to a great degree.

Well, I didn't intend to have off rhymes. It's just that you have to end a line with a word.

I don't mean end rhymes. But internally there are a lot of rhymes. You have puff and dust and up. . . . Short u and long o—alliteration—to get that exploding effect.

Whenever you want the intensity to increase—whenever the intensity does increase in human speech, it always turns out that there's some repetition of sound going on. It's no use to try to break the process down too carefully. It's just something that you notice happens. Then if you try to *gain* the intensity by *making* the sound repeat—that's backward. Anyway the idea is that assonance and all these things are helpful precisely because the psyche is interested in them. People do them naturally unless it's forbidden.

That's what we wanted to know. All that comes naturally? If you want to analyze those two lines further you have two anagrams.

What are anagrams?

The letters in "soul" are included in the word "slowly" and it makes a connection between the two. You have "up" in "puff." You have a shift in voice. You have all these images.

It's just like a dog barking. He doesn't know about anagrams.

That's our point. You did that just naturally. Or as a matter of craft being applied to the poem.

NO. No. No. Sometimes I'll—I don't remember when I wrote those exactly but I remember the sensation that they came out moderately whole. I worked with the last line for a long time to get the idea of a flat plain. I wanted the image of a flat plain as in a photograph of Kansas; on it would be a house that suddenly explodes. I thought of "Nebraska." I asked several people about the word Nebraska, and they said "I see mountains when I hear the word Nebraska." I never spoke to those people again. It wasn't a craft issue. But I know what you're getting at in a way, and I do think that if the human being learns to speak intensely . . . sometimes he learns to speak that way from his mother . . . sometimes from friends that speak more intensely then he. I was like that. . . .

Maybe from the teacher in his workshop?

Yeah. Maybe. I never heard a workshop person speak intensely except maybe John Logan and David Ray. Anyway, it's possible that this might happen. There are various ways a young poet can become aware of sound. It's an important realization and from that point on . . . suppose you do feel intensely but the line is flat. It's possible that in fact there *is* sound missing. There is strong sound missing. Missing it helps you understand why the line is bad. Otherwise it seems perfectly good. I agree with you that changes of sound are tremendously important in the whole flow of the poem. Still I resist the idea of naming them and going over them carefully and trying to apply them.

In the work of Robert Lowell he uses a great deal of imagination and images. And also his poetry is what one would call very well crafted. He has worked on that poetry in order to get that effect.

Oh, yes. Oh, yes indeed.

He doesn't have this spontaneity thing the way Ginsberg does.

Lord Weary's Castle is a work with powerful sound. He clearly spent hours and hours working on the sound in that book. It's one thing that I've always loved about the book. And those of us who were beginning to write at that time found a lot of sound work also in Richard Wilbur . . . in *The Beautiful Changes,* which came out the same year. So in a way we were sensitized to sound by these two books. I love both books still, but perhaps the sound is put together *too* architecturally . . . maybe there is some crafting of green wood going on. Maybe it would have been better if they had let the tree grow bigger first . . . Americans are impatient . . . I don't know where we are now. Voznesensky is apparently the greatest craftsman in the world, in terms of sound.

Yes. That's in the Russian?

That's in the Russian. And he does not craft it in any one way—only in iambic. And Brodsky is said to be fantastic in sound. Lowell does understand psychic energy. In cunning he's never been very good with that. He has never—I can't explain it, but you get the feeling that he's at parties too often. It's something neither Rilke nor Whitman were interested in. And in sound . . .

But he does exert craft. He is an excellent craftsman. . . .

In an interview in the *Paris Review,* Lowell said something like this: "I was a free verse poet, and on my honeymoon I pitched a tent on Tate's lawn, and in three weeks Tate turned me from a free verse poet into a rhymed iambic poet." Despite Lowell's excitement and Tate's intelligence, I get the impression that this was a disastrous turn of events. In Lowell's book you have sounds all clashing against each other. Exciting. Unfortunately this is mixed with old-fashioned attempts at meter and rhyme, sort of antique work.

The influence of Tate on Lowell you felt was disastrous at one time?

In that respect.

In that respect?

Yes. He taught Lowell to bring in the historical which Tate in turn had learned from Eliot. There's a heavy historical world in *Lord Weary's Castle.* There's that heavy clash of opinions in the book, and each "set" of opinions represents a different sort of psychic energy. He rather clumsily has them represented by the Roman Catholic Church on the one hand—good psychic energy—and the New England Protestants on the other—evil psychic energy. And this is a very rudimentary clash, but at least it's a clash. To me that clash is a modern clash, and yet all of it is somehow undermined by the seventeenth-century meter and rhyme which says: "Well, it's a game after all. I'm not living in this century after all. Goodbye." I don't know the man. I've never talked to him about these things. But I have the strong sensation that he felt there was something wrong with this overly architectural sound because in *Life Studies* he turned away from it completely, and wrote in a William-Carlos-Williams-influenced free verse. And Tate evidently said, "Do not publish *Life Studies.* It is a bad book."

It's none of my business, but I wish he had done a free verse book before his interest in sound diminished. If he had done a free verse book in 1947 with that magnificent sense of sound he had . . .

We don't think he loses his sense of sound in Life Studies.

What sense of sound he has is pedestrian. It's very useful for what he's doing. It's quite adapted to the content, but at the same time it's not lively. Much of the book is prose turned into poems; as you know, it was a prose document begun for his psychiatrist. It was not originally conceived as poetry. I just don't find the sound there exciting. It's useful but it's not exciting. And in his new book I don't find much sound at all.

Notebooks?

In *Notebooks* I don't find much sound at all. It's conceivable that in his *Notebooks* he has descended to a very rudimentary (bumpy) idea of craft . . . kind of bumpy rhythms without much sound—well—I don't know what I'm getting into here. But I don't find any sound in the *Notebooks* and I don't find any serious craft in the *Notebooks*. I see a tremendous amount of verbal manipulation done with the intelligence—but I don't find the sound expresses any psychic realities. It's as if they were living in separate places. There is the possibility that we are living in a time in which American poets actually ignore the whole matter of sound. Various excuses are brought up: because rhyme is really old-fashioned, because we don't have a meter, because William Carlos Williams is thought to have said "just use cat and dog language," because the Olsonites write too much, because earlier attempts at sound work appear at this moment to be failures—maybe they aren't. As a result of all this the connection between sound and psychic energy is never deeply investigated. The way Voznesensky has investigated it. The way Brodsky has. The way Lorca has investigated it. The way Trakl has investigated it. And we suspect that may be true when we hear so many poets read in a flat and dull voice. "I want the poem to stand on its own feet," they say, as if their voices were not feet. The voices are not clear. And then when you hear a Russian read, you think: My God, how powerful sound can be in a poem! And what Lorca and the Russians do is to worship and understand the sound element in a poem. They worship it. Ginsberg's record of Blake poems is powerful, too—in a different way. I like it.

S. G.: You know in Mann's Death in Venice, *Aschenbach had reached a point where he discovered that everybody was working on craft alone, and that is when he made the trip to Venice.*

That's very interesting.

S. G.: That's what happened to him. In your terms he went to the water place—Venice—to try to get his own tree to grow again.

Do you remember what Frost said, "Drink, and be whole again beyond confusion". . . . Well, all I've been doing is just repeating again and again the idea that all the traditional applications of the word craft have to be dropped. American craft-talk has been connected with the idea of the poem as a dead object, as a dead object and constructed.

But the whole genius of modern poetry lies in its grasp of flowing psychic energy.

Taking care of animals is the best preparation for writing poems. When you write poems, you feed poems language.

What would you substitute for the word "craft"?

I've already substituted: "letting the creature live." And

as soon as you ask: "Do you think synecdoche is useful in letting the creature live?" The answer is clear right away: Don't try to insert any plastic or aluminum pieces. It won't work. The creature will die. Understand me?

Yeah, yeah, we understand you.

Another way you could put it is that instead of talking about craft you could talk about intensiveness, alertness. We have lots of students in the workshops who are not alert.

About your recent poem —"The Teeth Mother Naked at Last"—will you explain the myth?

No, it takes too long. I have about twenty prose pages in my new book in which I go into the speculation that thousands of years of mother culture have come before us.

Can you tell us something about the crafting of "Teeth Mother"?

Nothing interesting in it except that I wrote it some-what with my voice—I spoke parts aloud at readings many times before I wrote them down. That's the only interesting thing. I'm still very dissatisfied with the way it looks on the page. It's okay for the voice. . . .

How are you dissatisfied?

I don't like the way it looks on the page.

The arrangement of the lines?

I'm just dissatisfied with the poem.

Is there anything you'd like to say that we haven't touched on?

Clearly, I don't believe in craft as a static discipline, but I do believe in hard work, and in a growth, as if by evolution, of poetry, which each poet lives through during the decades he is alive, whether he wants to or not, and which he can further or not, as he wishes.

In the late forties the conscious and the unconscious were brought together in Wilbur and Lowell in poetry of very high quality. In the last decade that union has fallen apart, I think because of an evolutionary need to emphasize images, which introduce new material from the unconscious. In this situation the conscious mind appears to retreat from the poem, and static form, or form by will, which the conscious mind is interested in, is ignored. But the evolutionary is still powerful in American poetry, and we don't know where this growth will embody itself next, just as the poets in the late forties could not predict the flooding in of material from the unconscious that was about to take place. I think the openness to the image will continue, and material from the far distant past of the psyche will begin to come in. I think there will be a lot of work on sound soon. A new organ will begin to pick up sound. That implies that the unconscious, which often channels itself into sound, will keep up its gifts—or its invasion—however you like to describe it! . . . The conscious mind is more confident of its ability to shape *sound* than its ability to shape the *image*. In Homer and Pindar you see the conscious and the unconscious working together on sound.

Hard work in a poet means inner psychic labor, what Tranströmer calls "working on himself," but also it means his or her attempt to share in or even encourage the movement into sound areas . . . what poetry longs to do. . . . We haven't gotten into these possibilities at all, but this interview is too long as it is, and I'm not what I've said in it. . . .

V

Talk about the "Great Mother"

The Masculine versus the
Feminine in Poetry
An Interview with William Heyen and
Gregory Fitz Gerald

Brockport, New York, Spring, 1970

Gregory Fitz Gerald: You speak about the "Great Mother" in your readings. How is that related to psychic energy in poetry?

The Great Mother was evidently the one "divine creature" of all early humanity, pervading everything. Neumann believes that it wasn't until 3000 or 2000 B.C. around the Mediterranean that Greek men began to escape from the mother goddess, and develop tiny threads of masculine consciousness. We who are now alive represent the tail end of a long development of masculine consciousness, a long flight from the mother goddess. The Mediterranean peoples, when they adopted Christianity, kept the Great Mother in the form of the Virgin Mary. But the farther north you go in Europe, the more fanatic the hatred of the Mother was. It's significant therefore that the Reformation began in Germany. What they did essentially was to get rid of the last remnant of the Great Mother, that is Mary; that was called the Reformation. And in New England the process continued. Max Weber pointed out how well capitalism and Puritanism went together. We've come to the end of that process now. At least American humanity has gone as far as it's going to go in the direction of masculine consciousness. This shows up in music and poetry.

G. F. G.: How does all this appear in poetry, and specifically, yours?

We notice the reappearance of the poetry of ecstasy. I feel it in Whitman, and sometimes in Wilbur. Then in Snyder, occasionally, in Ginsberg's chants and his Blake songs, in McClure, and the excitable poets. Father gods like it all dry and not too enthusiastic.

G. F. G.: What other characteristics of the mother goddess do you find in poetry?

In the fifties, when poets used iambic meter heavily, I sense that the poets experienced that as a triumph of masculine consciousness—meter imposing itself upon "material," which is basically feminine. What is happening today is the continuation of Whitman's free verse—which lets the feminine elements emerge in the poem, without trying to impose a masculine pattern upon them. Some checks and repressions have lightened.

G. F. G: Do you have a poem that you feel illustrates this influence?

Most of my poems in the last two years are no doubt linked to the thoughts I've had about the Mother. About ten years ago, before I had read Neumann or Jung on the subject, I wrote a poem which turned out to contrast mother and father consciousness. As a "speaker," I choose a businessman, or at least a busy man, who tells us what he thinks. The poem is called: "The Busy Man Speaks"

Not to the mother of solitude will I give myself
Away, not to the mother of love, nor to the mother of
    conversation,
Nor to the mother of art, nor the mother
Of tears, nor the mother of the ocean;
Not to the mother of sorrow, nor the mother
Of the downcast face, nor the mother of the suffering of
    death;
Not to the mother of the night full of crickets,
Nor the mother of the open fields, nor the mother of Christ

But I will give myself to the father of righteousness,
    the father
Of cheerfulness, who is also the father of rocks,
Who is also the father of perfect gestures;
From the Chase National Bank
An arm of flame has come, and I am drawn
To the desert, to the parched places, to the landscape
    of zeros;
And I shall give myself away to the father of righteousness,
The stones of cheerfulness, the steel of money, the father
    of rocks.

*G. F. G.: Is it accurate to say that you feel the masculine
principle is destructive?*

When it gets too far from the feminine, yes. Most western
men are. But masculine consciousness in itself is not evil.
Far from it. In its highest levels, it is pure light. There
must be a balance between two poles of consciousness.
Before and during the Middle Ages Celts and Gauls were
moving into masculine consciousness, keeping a tremen-
dous amount of feminine consciousness. The Cathedral
of Chartres is deeply feminine. At the same time, a great
masculine drive built it. But as you follow history to the

present day you begin to suspect that unbalanced masculine consciousness constantly "overreacts," it overwins, destroys the balance of power. Finally, being separated too far from their own feminine consciousness, men, as political animals, go insane.

William Heyen: To switch ground a little bit, it was in 1956, wasn't it, that you went to Norway on a Fulbright to do some translating? And it was there that you happened to discover poets like Neruda, Trakl, and Vallejo? What was it about these poets that made them seem important to you?

I went to Oslo, and in the Oslo library, I found translations of Neruda. And I'll never forget the first line of Neruda I saw. It went something like this: "Young girls, with their hands on their hearts, dreaming of pirates." It's a lovely line—both in the willingness to like young girls and in the freedom to bring the willingness into an "interior" poem. Pulling in the pirates made it a wonderful world.

When you get into the work of Neruda and Vallejo you find a great enthusiasm for energy itself, for women, for an exuberant life that's not in Pound or Eliot. That's what I found.

W. H.: It's a new sense of association. A kind of imagery that visits a lot of different worlds at once.

I'm trying to write some prose for the next issue of my magazine, which will touch on the new brain research being done by Paul MacLean and others. There these "different worlds" appear as "different brains." The scary detail is that these brains appear to have, in normal life, no central organization. There is no one dominant

"I." Robinson Crusoe is not actually Robinson Crusoe. Robinson feels he is one person, because his parents called him "Robinson," and he keeps looking for the unity he thinks should be there. He then feels a need to impose unity everywhere. The man with overly masculine consciousness has a fanatical need to unite himself. In poetry this overly masculine consciousness works hard to impose an oversimplified unity on the poem. If the images don't fit, he throws them out, until he gets a unified, if limited, whole. That's not what Lorca, Vallejo, and Neruda do. They try to bring in images from many worlds, to open the poem again to abundance, so that its variety suggests the abundance inside our own heads.

G. F. G.: Other than this work on the brain, what has the magazine been doing lately?

Nothing, lately. I started the magazine *The Fifties* about 1958, and we then spent time attacking academic poets. Then I put it out through the sixties, mainly for two reasons: to bring in European poets like Neruda and Vallejo, whom other editors were not publishing, and also to publish articles on some of the younger poets. I'm continuing this policy into the seventies. But it's my own magazine; I put it out when I feel like it; and I put it out once every year, once every year and a half—it doesn't matter to me. Subscribers have to wait. My wife's idea is that when someone subscribes to *The Sixties* we ought to ask for the next of kin, because the subscriber may die before he gets his next issue.

W. H.: I've been delighted by The Morning Glory, *your twelve prose poems. Does working in that form enable you to "break out" a little bit more?*

I like the prose poem. It's odd that we have so few prose poems in English. The Spanish and the French have lovely ones.

W. H.: It's a genre that has always made the American academic uncomfortable. We want to see those lines, the left-hand margin ought preferably to be even.

Writing them, we don't worry about where the line ends!

G. F. G.: What you've been saying about the psychic energy relates, no doubt, to what the critics have discussed as the "deep image." Ralph Mills says that you are one of a group of poets who

> *mold their work around a group of images deriving from subliminal regions of the mind, and joined by association of an emotional, symbolic, and lyrical kind. Each poem seems to mirror a condition of intense subjectivity, a moment of extreme perception, personal to the poet, and yet capable of stirring subtle and profound responses in the reader.*

What he says is not untrue. Antonio Machado says:

> Mankind owns four things
> that are no good at sea:
> rudder, anchor, oars
> and the fear of going down.

Wonderful poem.

Edited from a videotape interview with Robert Bly in the Spring, 1970, sponsored by the Brockport Writers Forum, Department of English, State University College, Brockport, N.Y. 14420 © State University of New York.

About the Conference on the Mother

An Interview with Bill Siemering

Moorhead, Minnesota, May, 1975

I wonder why this suppression of the woman in society. Why is woman so feared by men?

No one knows about that. There are several possibilities. A historical view would be that under the matriarchies the men themselves were oppressed. Men had a "men's liberation society" for four hundred thousand years. And maybe around 2000 B.C.—somewhere in there—the men finally organized. The Jews were very strong in that "society," and the Old Testament describes how you eradicate a Great Mother. Her name evidently in Hebrew was Deborah—the bee. The mother is often associated with the queen bee. Deborah was destroyed and Jehovah's marriage with her broken. There is some vindictiveness on the part of the men, and I think it may come from the old matriarchies. I don't know. Also I think there's a fear on the men's part of their own female side.

And the creative is frequently suspect too, then, being part of the female side.

Rumi, the Persian poet thinks so. One of his poems associates creativity firmly with the female soul. I don't believe a man can be creative with his male side only. I found that out myself. I was brought up in the patriarchy of the Middle West. I was a Lutheran besides; and then I went to college. On the whole the colleges are father oriented, except for a rare teacher. And then I tried to write poetry, using only my right side, evidently, using only father consciousness as I had been taught. It was impossible. The poetry I wrote was worthless. But in the normal course of events, a man in his late twenties, or early thirties, will start to come toward mother consciousness on his own. Solitude is valuable in starting that movement, and deepening it. I found that to be the case. I wasn't surprised when I read in Robert Graves's *Greek Myths* that the word "muse" is an archaic Greek word for the moon! Evidently it is an old word for the mother, or for mother consciousness. So the patriarchal Greeks of 700 B.C. would begin a poem by saying, "Mother consciousness, please come and help me with this poem!"

How do you go about having people become more aware of mother consciousness?

Inside of them?

Yes.

Well, Lorca always uses the word, "I want," or the phrase, "I want, I desire," "I want you green, be more green." ". . . The ship on the sea and the horse on the mountain." The whole idea of our desires and our loves and our affections and our ecstasies lie really on our mother-consciousness side. Perhaps you forget about rules, and return to the ancient idea of consulting yourself *inside,* as Blake says. If you neglect that consultation, you turn into standing water, and Blake says, "Expect poison from standing water."

The *Tao Te Ching* talks about the return to the mother, and it says, "The top of the mountain"—that is the father consciousness—"is good." But what's really interesting happens at the base, in the shadows of the mountains. The *Tao Te Ching* says, "The spokes of the wheel are good, but the wheel is only useful because of the hollow space at the center." It says, "Know the male, but cling to the female, and be the river valley of the world." How an adult male "returns" is your question. Meditation of course is very helpful in all return to the mother. Once a man sits in the meditative position, he is sitting in the fetal position. Then the masculine consciousness is unable to go out and conquer Africa. Sometimes, a man may find his mother consciousness, which he's been out of touch with since he was five or six years old, rising in meditation. Women often find something similar—that their top-of-the-mountain consciousness that they've been out of touch with directly since they were five or six years old begins to rise in meditation. So those are practical things that people do.

Are those ways that you've gotten in touch with the female side of yourself?

Yes, in my case it was a matter of desperation, I suppose, because I found myself unable to continue. . . . unable to write, really. Poetry and all art is very useful in that way, because using only one side of your brain, you come up against a stone wall, and the man or woman won't be able to develop until he or she develops the missing side. I felt a *need* for solitude, and then I felt a *need* for meditation. I finally got some instructions from the Tibetans, who are very good in the development of both sides. And then of course, just as women are helped tremendously by men who respect their male consciousness, so tremendous help has been given to me by my wife who respected my female consciousness, what there was of it. Women writers help tremendously. The Swiss writer Marie Louise von Franz is an example of that.

Your Great Mother Conference is a fascinating prospect; and one gets down to some of the root causes of some of the problems, and really at some solutions perhaps. Change will not take place unless there's a change inside people. Laws can only legislate to a degree equal rights for people, but unless people's hearts are changed and minds are changed, why . . .

Everyone feels a great longing, you know, to live with more depth.

With wholeness too.

Yes. Well, we are doing this conference on a shoestring, with no money at all. Foundation support would be far too much a father influence, I think, and we don't plan to make any money out of it either. It will last ten to twelve days; some people will camp, others live in cabins in the mountains; each person will pay ten dollars a day for it all, including food and lodging. If we have any money left at the end it will be redistributed. That seems to be an idea of the mother too.

What will you do during the day?

I don't know, that's one of the things that we will think about there. This practical issue of daily life—what has happened to us is that the positive mother energy around us has become completely invisible. And men are generally afraid of all women.

Why is that?

I think because they don't separate out the negative and the positive. In ancient times, for example, in the ancient matriarchies, women and men would divide mother energy into good mother energies, for one example, and death energies, death mothers. In India, where they've kept a great deal of mother consciousness, they still worship Kali, the Death Mother. People in ancient times declared that certain women do have death mother energies in them. Hemingway's mother, for example, was evidently a death mother. You probably know the story of the pistol. When he was about twenty-six, he got a letter from his mother and a package. There was a pistol inside. Also a note saying, "Dear Ernest, this is the pistol your father shot himself with. I thought you'd like to have it." One reason both women and men were not as afraid in ancient times is that instead of maintaining that the gentleness of the Virgin Mary is the essence of all women, they said, "No, there are negative energies . . . there are extremely destructive women, exactly as there are extremely destructive men." And you must learn to be sensitive to these death energies, and once you learn to be sensitive to them, you won't be afraid in general of all women. You become sensitive to the good energy too. They worked to visualize, with sculpture and "myth" both sorts of female energy or mother consciousness, and so helped men and women to see it all much more clearly. Neither men nor women see these things now as clearly as they did in ancient times.

And men are vulnerable. And therefore sometimes overly defensive. . . .

They're vulnerable because they've been standing on one leg for a long time—on their patriarchal leg. And a heron on one leg can easily be pushed over.

We've kind of reached the peak, then, in our society, in America particularly in industrialist society: the patriarchal society, the authoritarian, the father god.

Many seem to feel—as I know you do—that this patriarchal society is collapsing. It's collapsing partly because of poor decisions being made by males in government matters. From the point of view of consciousness, statesmen make these errors because they actually are living in an unbalanced consciousness, with much too much of father consciousness and too little of the mother consciousness. I am not saying that father consciousness is bad, and mother consciousness is good. Both consciousnesses are marvelous. But when you go as far as we have in despising women and fearing female consciousness, which also means fearing the female part of a man, at that point you can't help but have an imbalance, which would lead you to disasters.

And perhaps the Vietnam war is a culmination of that kind of consciousness.

It's quite possible that the country of Vietnam represents to us the mother consciousness. The patriarchies wobble, they become more and more desperate; perhaps they have a simple hatred for all forms of mother consciousness.

That is, we really don't have justice; there isn't equal justice under the law. We talk about peace with honor in Vietnam, and I don't think there was either peace or much honor for the people there, or for ourselves. And so there's a lot of crumbling of myth. David Halberstam has a recent article on the fall of Vietnam in the New Times, *and he talks about the final end of this myth of supremacy, the myth that we have unlimited power, that we can do everything.*

That myth is a wonderful righthand obsession.

How is the change going to affect Americans in their own self-concepts?

You mean the collapse of the patriarchies?

Right.

It's going to harm the self-esteem of men.

The ego?

The ego. But the ego can link itself to anything. In the patriarchies, evidently, it tends to link itself with objects, with deeds, with property. It is receiving less and less support from these objects. But it can link itself with the universe. Since much of the universe is joyful, the ego then becomes joyful. That was the hope under the matriarchies. And we have to hope that will happen again, in a contemporary form.

And what about men? Will they be less concerned about climbing the corporate ladder, the hierarchical kind of thing?

Obsessive competitiveness is a right-sided thing, involving domination of the earth, as ecology has shown, instead

of living *with* it. Thoreau had a lot of mother conscious-
ness in him, and he developed it further by living with
Mother Nature. In religion, father consciousness shows
itself usually through morality and rules. When Moses
comes down, he has a series of tablets, given him by the
Father God which says, "Don't do this, and don't do
that, and don't do this and don't do that." Blake tries
to explain the opposite of that in *The Marriage of Heaven
and Hell.* We'd love to imagine tablets that say: "Do
make love." "Do go out and kiss a tree." "Energy is
eternal delight."

In body motion, father consciousness often shows
itself in stiffness, inability to move the hands, holding
the body tight. In the patriarchy both men and women
worship the divine by sitting stiffly in a chair or in a
pew. In the matriarchy, there was a sense no human be-
ing could worship the divine unless his or her body is
moving. So dance was present! We've asked Ann Igoe
from Charleston to come and teach us dancing each day,
and she has agreed.

Art held off the father for a long time, but it finally
gave in, with academic art, and hard line art, where you
have nothing but straight lines, and solid blocks of rec-
tangular color. All these contrasts are full of energy.
Rita Schumaker from North Carolina will be our teacher
in drawing and painting, and never having done any
drawing or painting, I look forward to that!

*We have that notion, though, that the female is soft,
gentle, and so on, and therefore the male consciousness
calls it weak. By contrast, in Eastern thought, in the* Tao
Te Ching, *there's the idea of water as gentleness, but
also as great strength.*

Historians suspect that in matriarchies, women run the

religious and political life, and created the myths. Their way of growth produced tremendous character. So that the female energy at that time was extremely powerful. One of the things we are going to talk about is the possibility that *The Odyssey* is a secret text from late mother times. Far from being an epic about a warrior civilization, *The Odyssey* actually describes how to deal with enormous concentrations of female energy, both negative and positive. Each island visited embodies a different concentration of energy, some of them destructive to women as well as to men, and some of them not.

But we shouldn't have to deal in this either / or all the time; isn't there a chance for synthesis? We do have two sides of our brain, after all.

Yes, I think so. You're referring to the new brain research, indicating one lobe is basically logical, the other emotional. . . . And in the brain there is provision for a great deal of flow back and forth between these two lobes of the brain, or forms of consciousness. I agree that the disintegration of the patriarchy does not mean we will return to the matriarchy. Both men and women have been changed in the meantime. A matriarchy became firmly established centuries ago. Then a patriarchy became firmly established. So it appears the next step is a union of the two, of some sort, of some unknown kind.

A new wholeness.

Yes. One way that it can be described is that when the mother has become creative again, a spiritual child will be born. But that is beyond our conference really; what we're trying to do really is to study the contrasts between the two sorts of consciousness. Robert Sadin, who directs the symphony and choruses at the University of Cincinnati, has noticed this contrast coming forward in Mahler. Robert noticed that for his Eighth Symphony, he provided alternating texts, one in German, the other in Latin, one embodying mother consciousness, the other father consciousness. So Robert Sadin will play music indicating how the contrasts, or unions, appear in music. For my part, I want to teach a course on the fairy story. It's primarily to introduce some ideas of a woman I find fantastically intelligent, Marie Louise von Franz, who is sixty years old this year. She lives in Zurich. She believes that the fairy stories contain in them a tremendous amount of ancient knowledge about the growth of the male and female sides of people. She draws from the tales amazing insights on what the process of growth in a woman is like. Her book *The Feminine in Fairy Tales* is brilliant, a great book. So we'll be discussing her ideas.

I believe you have a new manuscript from biblical days.

Thank you, I'd forgotten that for a moment. A manuscript in old Slavonic was found in the Hapsburg Libraries, *The Essene Gospel of Christ,* which may or may not be an Essene Gospel. The gist of the Gospel is Christ's care to provide forms of worship for the Earthly Mother as well as the Heavenly Father. It's possible the patriarchal Christians who came later suppressed much of this material. Christ himself defends mother consciousness, as He shows with His refusal to stone the woman in adultery. This is what a Mother's Prayer might sound like: "Our Mother who art in earth, your name was always holy. Your Kingdom has already arrived here in the body. May we sense what the whole universe wants to be, both in the body and in the spirit. May we make our own bread every day, and may we forgive everyone, even those who have not transgressed against us. Do not lead us into sickness, and save us from the longing we have to damage ourselves. For the body is yours, and delight, and ecstasy, forever and ever. Amen."

On Split-Brain Experiments and the Mother

An Interview with Kevin Powers

Buffalo, New York, April, 1974

Do you think that America is in a position now that is destructive, that there's a domination now of the "Death Mother," of Kali?

As the patriarchy begins to fail, the old Mothers come forward; and so the Death Mother comes forward.

Is there a move in your work from Demeter in Silence in the Snowy Fields *to Kali?*

If a man's own mother was a "good mother," then the "Good Mother" is the first of the "goddesses" he becomes aware of. I became aware of Demeter values first, I guess, like Gary Snyder. Gradually, as you get older, you become aware of some of the other mothers. And some of the other Fathers.

Is that awareness of the Death Mother any kind of death wish?

I don't think so! You know Freud considered in the

first half of his life Eros energy to be the most powerful energy in the unconscious; we could also call that Demeter energy or Good Mother energy. Then, during the First World War, he saw Europe committing suicide, and it came to him that there is another balancing energy involved, which might be called the Death Wish, or the desire to die.

One could say that not being aware of the Death Wish opens you to the Death Mother! Freud's "error" was curiously like Europe's.

The Indians consider Kali an ecstatic and sensual kind of energy as well. . . .

Yes.

Is meditation a way to use Kali's sensual energy as a form of sublimation?

I'm not old enough yet to really use Kali in an ecstatic way, but the Indians have always said that any one of the Mothers will expand and include the other Mothers. Artemis, for example, evidently begins as an Ecstatic Mother, yet gradually she expands and includes Demeter values and finally becomes a Great Mother, in that sense including all four Mothers.

Certainly I know that Eastern people, particularly Tibetans, always include the Death Mother in their meditation, and its effect apparently is to increase their energy and concentration.

Why are you interested in de Kooning?

Well, de Kooning is a contemporary artist in whom what

could be called the Negative Psychic Mother, the Teeth Mother, or the Stone Mother, appears. The hard lines of Mondrian . . . the chances are the hard lines mean also the Teeth Mother appearing, you just see the lines of the tooth.

I'd never thought of that. I'd always seen the horizontal and vertical as man and landscape, or as man and woman oppositions.

I don't know. But in Rembrandt, by contrast, you feel the Ecstatic Mother and the Demeter Mother (*The Woman Taking a Bath*). In much modern painting the Death Mother comes forward, and the Teeth Mother, from underneath, to disintegrate the painting.

De Kooning made an effort to destroy the woman figure later, isn't that related?

There is terror in all of this, so we have a great deal of antiwoman art and antiwoman literature taking place. It's not directed against women, but is a response to fear of interior, ignored Kalis, I think.

It would appear that the initial error was the decision in Roman times to adore only the Virgin Mary. . . .

You've called the breath the deepest evolutionary link our body has and Snyder talks of breath as spirit, making a distinction between inspiration, the world coming into the body, and expiration, which he says is voiced as a signal for the species to connect. Would you accept this sort of distinction?

Lovely idea! Lovely idea! So if one wants to meditate on life and death, all one has to do is breathe. Evidently the ancient Vedic meditators agreed. I like Gary Snyder's attentiveness very much.

And would you think therefore that if we follow Snyder through, that the inspiration we're taking at the moment, the breathing in, has become a creative problem because essentially what we're breathing in is destructive.

You're enlarging the meaning of "breathing in" now. The Vedic people speak of breath, that's all. Do you mean polluted air?

Yes, polluted air, but also the social and psychological environment.

Well, breathing means that we pull in thousands of particles of energy that we are not aware of. Some teachers taught that you have to work for years before you take your first breath, which means . . . I don't know what it means, but it does say something about learning to draw this energy into the psyche. Now one reason that you would draw that in, and hold it there, is to prevent the destructive elements of the society from coming in.

Last night at your reading you were talking of another neurological theory. You were talking about the division into left and right. How does that relate to the earlier brain theories?

I don't know. These are two separate streams of brain work. Robert Ornstein's book, *The Psychology of Consciousness,* reports on the so-called split-brain experiments done in recent years. We have left and right brains; and it turns out there is a crossover system. Doctors have known that for years, because if a person has a stroke in the right brain, it affects the left side of the body, and vice versa. The new material came from investigations of persons whose right and left brains were severed.

The connection had been severed?

Yes, exactly. By studying the "half-brains" separately, they found out that the left side of the brain (controlling the right side of the body) is basically rational, logical, and linear. It is involved in time. Probably it is the superego Freud talked about. Then the right side of the brain (that controls the left side of the body) is intuitive; it is emotional and associational, it has values we call "feminine"; it deals with space, not time. Language on the whole seems to belong primarily to the right side, the logical side, of the body. Grammar appears to have a logical basis.

Anyway, the brain investigators at one point ask a question of the brain, and then ask the left hand to write the answer. The person involved has had the connection between the two brains severed in an accident. The movie of this scene shows the left hand slowly and laboriously beginning to write the answer, and suddenly the right hand sweeps in, knocks the left hand away, grabs the pencil and writes the answer. The movie is evidently quite frightening. It reminds me of the "Beowulf action"; the men breaking the matriarchies and taking power.

You can also see a movie in which a man with split-brain has become angry. The man's left arm lifts up an ax, and is about to bring it down, suddenly the right hand sweeps in again, and holds the arm this time, preventing it from coming down. That scene appears to be a narrative in which the superego intervenes to prevent the id from taking an action. That scene suggests the possibility that the patriarchies were developed to control the wild angers of the matriarchies.

No one can read these experiments without realizing how much we need both "sides" . . . in recent years, both men and women have been reluctant to respect the male side.

Did you find there was a serious problem in introducing political language because that language belongs to a system which in fact you're not in sympathy with, and that system has appropriated the meaning of language and neutralized it and milked it?

Yes, I find great difficulty in it. And some of my political poems are failures also.

You've juxtaposed in earlier poems a political word with another word that comes from a more vital source in order to give that political word new energy. But I notice in "The Teeth Mother Naked at Last" you use flatter statements without this juxtaposition.

That is complicated. In one passage of "The Teeth Mother" I mentioned that the pilots bomb "huts," afterward described as "structures." So in that line you can see that the technocrats have withdrawn energy from the word "structures" in order to tell lies about what they are doing. You have to be aware of who is withdrawing energy from a word before you put it into a poem, otherwise it'll withdraw energy from your poem. Since so many words have had their energy corrupted, it's very difficult to write poetry, and I'm not surprised that people work five to six months on a single short poem, I do myself. Some words are still rich and abundant. But millions of people spend their entire lives with words from which other people have withdrawn the energy.

You've said that you're interested in the rhythms of the ordinary spoken language and that normally the line is a controlling feature of the poem with you. Is there a danger now that within America ordinary speech rhythm itself is getting an artificial kind of energy?

Give me an example.

Well, the sort of energy they can put into short prepositions and make them appear weighted and philosophic, you're really into it, you're at it, you're with it. They've charged them inside with a higher possibility than the preposition will really allow.

Very interesting. . . . It's possible that the de-energizing of language by the technocrats and the bureaucrats is pressing in on the speaker, and in a way he takes a small pocket of language and saves it by investing all of his energy into it. It's ambiguous. It's a little like putting all your energy into a miniscule garden plot in the center of a skyscraper complex.

Could you say how the reverberations of the images function in a poem. Is it a combination of meaning and sound? Which do you feel has the greatest cutting edge?

I don't know about that. . . .

You've made a distinction between surrealism and false surrealism . . . could you go on with that . . . ?

Lately I've thought there may be something we could call a false unconscious. We're not quite aware of it yet. There are many poets writing in France, in England, in the United States, in Germany who turn out image after image, and yet the images do not refer solidly to anything in our psyche, so evidently they're not coming from the unconscious. This kind of stuff is all around us in the magazines. The images *appear* to be images, they *appear* to have unconscious substance, and yet they do not connect to our lives.

What is happening? The rational mind of the Western man evidently has begun to make up images that resemble images from the unconscious. It's the same process that takes place when a factory makes a plastic table that imitates a wooden table. . . . I saw recently a small desert scene on a sidetable . . . the man had been to the desert . . . several cactuses, rocks, sand . . . even the sand was plastic!

We know that process is taking place all the time in the outer world. I think the process is now taking place in the inner world too.

That would explain your attitude to French surrealism. The fact that French surrealists were living inside an urban environment under tension would tend to make them produce images from what you call the false unconscious?

Breton in many of his images reaches down and touches something genuine. I don't think that many surrealists follow him in that. Very few people agree with me on that point!

The New York school would then be throwing up false images, according to your definition, because they live in this environment which is antagonistic to a man finding his realized imaginative self. But isn't this environment a natural and organic extension of American culture?

It's an inorganic extension. Great poetry has come from the Andalusian countryside in this century, modern poetry. Lorca's is an example, and some of Juan Ramon Jimenez's. I have the sense that the feelings leave Juan Ramon's body, go out into the countryside, and return. A circuit is completed. A poet in an American city sends his feelings out, they hit an ugly parking lot, and don't come back. New York has a marvelous poet, David Ignatow. Perhaps his poems don't go out into the city, but out into people.

Do you think one possible answer to this is what Rothenberg is doing—an immersion into ritual and into a smaller community where the poet and his voice are more able to maintain contact with the group, i.e., poet as shaman?

What do you mean exactly?

Well, his movement toward primitive verse, his chanting, his use of repetitive sequences and chance techniques—all indicate a sense of rebuilding from base, a restoring of the tribal unit.

I have several inconsistent thoughts on that. We're not feeling each other any more in big groups, and that recognition in Jerry Rothenberg's work I like very much. I like the attention to non-English sound patterns. But from another point of view there's something goofy about the Western man saying, "I'm a poet and therefore I'm half Seneca Indian already. I'm an Eskimo!" Let the Eskimos say that.

David Ignatow says, "I am a city person and I'm sur-

232

rounded by thousands of angry human beings and I am an angry and furious human being. What do I do now?" I feel somehow that leads farther than for a Westernized man to say, "I'm getting shamanized. Pretty soon I'll be an Indian." Gary Snyder says that too sometimes.

But isn't Rothenberg's point that it isn't a move back, or "becoming an Eskimo," but a new allocation of energies. Isn't living in the primitive perpetual present now a meaningful and relevant concept?

It's too intellectual. How could we will ourselves to live in the perpetual present? The "primitive" does not will that; he is just in it. Our culture has the possibility of a perpetual present in it, hidden. But attempting to write primitive poetry is just a distraction.

What would your attitude be toward Roscwicz who said, "What I produce is poetry for the horror stricken. For those abandoned to butchery. For survivors. We learned poetry from scratch those people and I." What are your comments on his antipoetry and his distrust of the image?

I like the old English phrase, "True for you." There's a great power thrust in his sentences. I think there are still many people in society more whole than the poets. Poetry I think is a healing process, and when a person tries to write poetry with depth, he will find himself guided along paths that will heal him; and his presence on those paths is more important actually than any of the poetry that he writes. If our society were strong and spiritually healthy, it would heal us. But our society is not like that, so each person has to do most of the spiritual work himself. Tranströmer speaks of the need for each person to "do work on himself." I believe in that.

> Task: to be where I am.
> Even when I'm in this solemn and absurd
> role: I am still the place
> where creation does some work on itself.

Here's a Rilke poem to end with:

I live my life in growing orbits,
which move out over the things of the world.
Perhaps I can never achieve the last,
but that will be my attempt.

I am moving around God, around the ancient tower,
and I have been circling for a thousand years.
And I still don't know if I am a falcon,
or a storm, or a great song.

Three Poems

Clouds Grow Heavy

Clouds grow heavy; thunder goes.
Rain drives in from the east, its patter falls on the sides
    of houses.
Rain can be destructive, wiping out boundary marks.
But the soil needs care—ecstatic love has sprouts now,
    and renunciation.
Let the rain feed both.
Only the farmer with intelligence actually brings his
    harvest back to his farmyard.
He will fill the granary bins, and feed both the wise men
    and the saints.

Kabir
Version by R. B.

The Drunkards Are Arriving

The drunkards are rolling in slowly, those who hold to
wine are approaching.
The lovers come, singing, from the garden, the ones with
brilliant eyes.

The I-don't-want-to-lives are leaving, and the I-want-to-
lives are arriving.
They have gold sewn into their clothes, sewn in for those
who have none.

Those with ribs showing who have been grazing in the old
pasture of love
are turning up fat and frisky.

The souls of pure teachers are arriving like rays of
sunlight
from so far up to the ground-huggers.

How marvelous is that garden, where apples and pears,
both for the sake of the two Marys,
are arriving even in winter.

Those apples grow from the Gift, and they sink back
into the Gift.
It must be that they are coming from the garden to the
garden.

Rumi
Version by R. B.

Bread

My poems resemble the bread of Egypt—
one night passes over it, and you can't eat it any more.

Gobble it up now, while it's still fresh,
before the dust settles on it.

The place where a poem belongs is the warmth of the
    chest,
out in the world it dies of cold.

Go ahead, put a fish on dry land,
it quivers for a few minutes, and then it is still.

And even if you eat my poems while they're fresh,
you still have to bring forward many images yourself.

Actually, my friend, what you're eating is your own
    imagination.
These poems are not just a bunch of old proverbs.

                          Rumi
                          Version by R. B.

VI

Recent Interviews

The Ascending Energy Arc

Answers to Students' Questions,
Suffolk County Community College

March, 1975

You said once that anyone who was going to write should go live alone for two years and not talk to anyone. Do you still feel the same way?

A person cannot write poetry unless he or she is on the ascending energy arc. We have these times in our lives, in which a little shock comes through and we see how we could be happier, or we could have more energy, and because those little peaks—and they're always accompanied by a certain elation, joy, escstasy—beautiful important moments at which you're hitting your peak. Those are the moments out of which a poem should come. So you don't forget that peak. If you pay attention to that peak it may return, and you'll begin to evolve, hum, with more energy all the time. Poetry has to do with those moments and if you betray those moments by trying to get your poems in the *New Yorker,* or to be famous with them, or to make money with them, you're going to destroy your own peak moments.

The whole capitalist system, we know, is against those peak moments; if you're working on the production line you have to leave it. And all capitalism tries to dull you with television so you don't recognize your own peak moments when they come. . . .

Finally, your unconscious says, "The hell with this guy, this person's a creep, I'm going back in the seed, I'll be reborn, better luck next time, I hope in New Guinea!" And what you should be trying to do in life is to prevent your unconscious from making that decision. To me this is what poetry is involved with. Anybody at his peak moment, who wants to sit down and write a poem, can write it, if he can get Keats and Wordsworth and Shakespeare, all that stuff out of his head. I'm not saying they're bad, they're great—Wordsworth unbelievably graceful! The point is, each one of us has our own psychic rhythms; and you can be confused by the poetic rhythms of English speech that you pick up from reading poetry in school. That's what blocks you from writing poetry at your peak moments. So you have to learn to love that, and let it go.

Why do we take them in all our poetry classes?

Because you're too lazy to read them on your own, that's why! You don't really love a poet until you've got him all alone by yourself. I had Wordsworth all alone by myself one time, when I was alone for about three or four weeks, and I just love him.

In what we call primitive tribes, everyone writes their poetry. They don't have someone like me come up and talk about poetry. Everyone does it on Saturday night. They get together and dance and write it. What happens to a man then, is that he agrees sometimes to go into solitude and remain there a while. That is Thoreau's message, that's also the message of St. John of the Cross, San Juan de la Cruz, and every other so-called mystic that we've ever had. It doesn't mean they're mystic at all, it means they have common sense, that's all.

. . . Here's some more advice. . . . You should work for a couple of years before you get married, both men and women. Feel what it's like to get a job and get the crummy check at the end of the time. Feel how crummy it is to get home at five. You already know that, eh?

Anthony Machado, the Spanish poet, has a beautiful little poem:

> How strange! Both of us
> with our instincts. . . .
> Suddenly we are four.

Each man has a female soul as well as a male soul, and each woman a male soul as well as a female soul. So when each of those has been encouraged and developed, a couple is four persons!

After my wife and I were married we lived on a farm where we still live, in Minnesota; and then I had time to be alone near trees. We both had. You see trees have only one side, the left side. . . . Maybe that's true. . . . What a good idea! That's why animals are so wonderful. That's why in ancient times human beings grew much more than they grow now, because in the Middle Ages, for example, if you went out to spend two hours in a barn everyday with animals, your left side was helped to grow fast. . . . Growth of the left side is linked to physical labor, to walking, to working outdoors. . . .

It's better for you to walk nine hundred miles to see one small Rembrandt painting in some cabin in Montana, than for you to take a train to the Metropolitan Museum and see twenty-four huge Rembrandts, because in the second case you've taken a subway and gone to a museum. You think that's how he got there? . . . Riding? . . . So what's wrong with suffering? Anyway, who are we as human beings to say we don't suffer? We have no right, no cause to suffer? We have ecstatic nerve endings, we have pain nerve endings. You try to use only the ecstatic ones and I guarantee you you'll end up as a lump. If you don't use your suffering nerve endings, life will force you to do it. It'll give you a husband who'll beat the hell out of you. And that'll be real pain. If you open yourself to suffering, the suffering will come through and maybe change into joy shortly afterward. If you try to block the suffering out and say, "I don't want to suffer, if I have to suffer to be a poet, I don't want to be a poet," that means I don't want to be a human being. Advertising urges you to say that.

Then the suffering waits around in the unconscious, and it says, "You don't want me, huh? Okay, dad, you don't like me, what do you think I am? Slap! That's for you. Slap! Cancer? Would you like that? Slap! I can't hear you. Huh? You want a wife who'll bitch at you all the time, I'll give you that." I'm serious, these things exist in the unconscious and you can't fool with them. You can push them away all you want to and they'll come right back. The best thing to do is to open yourself to it.

At your age, for example, I know what that feeling is, not wanting to go down in depression. But it's best to allow yourself to sink, let yourself go down into it. You want to hear a poem I wrote about depression? No, you don't want to? When I was in college all the poets were supposed to be happy—get a little iambic pentameter, that'll cheer you up, da dum da dum da dum da dum de dum. Later I realized that I was sad, so I said alright I'll write a poem on depression, why not? This is as good a subject for poems as a horse. So I wrote this poem, "Depression." In the second stanza I describe a dream—we were talking about that on the way here, letting go of the armor, and letting yourself go down.

I felt my heart beat like an engine high in the air,
Like those scaffolding engines standing only on planks;
My body hung about me like an old grain elevator,
Useless, clogged, full of blackened wheat.
My body was sour, my life dishonest, and I fell asleep.

I dreamt that men came toward me, carrying thin wires;
I felt the wires pass in, like fire; they were old Tibetans,
Dressed in padded clothes, to keep out cold;
Then three work gloves, lying fingers to fingers,
In a circle, came toward me, and I awoke.
Now I want to go back among the dark roots;
Now I want to see the day pulling its long wing;
I want to see nothing more than two feet high;
I want to see no one, I want to say nothing,
I want to go down and rest in the black earth of silence.

People have mentioned to me, you know there's a strong
suicide thing in this, huh? Yeah, that's right, but the
funny thing is I felt very good when I finished this. You
couldn't have got me to commit suicide for all the money
in the world.

I don't know what the dream meant at the end. But
John Logan said to me one time, "You know those
padded clothes that you have in that dream? What does
that mean?" I just had an image of a Chinaman with his
padded clothes, and I said, "I don't know, John, I had
the dream and put it in the poem." But he said, "It's
connected to the poem because this is a padding to keep
feeling out." And then I felt a flow and said, "That's
true, it could be called padded clothes to keep out pain."

Those three work gloves lying in a circle: physical
work helps your left side to grow, and, as a shape, the
circle is feminine. So what was coming toward me were

three work gloves, three ways of working physically, giving up all the mental cheerfulness. That's why I was happy when I finished the poem.

How do you feel about someone enjoying your poetry but getting a totally different interpretation of it?

It doesn't matter, it doesn't matter a bit. You interpret it according to what stage you are at, at that moment. And then as you go on, ten years from now you'll read the same poem and say, "Isn't that weird. I thought it was that way, but it's obviously this way." That's alright, you're unconsciously looking for printouts of your insight. Look for it anywhere, it doesn't matter. A true poem is written with the psyche underneath; it may have layers like a dream.

Then you say there's no right or wrong?

There's no right or wrong. When you go into a classroom with a small poem and talk about it, and bring it out into the body, relate it to your lives, you will be just amazed; everyone will have taken that poem and related it to his own deepest problem. They've taken that little beam of light and broken it up into its separate components, and everyone of us does that. That's why it's so horrible in high school when they say, "What's the interpretation of this poem? No, you're wrong, you're wrong."

Yeah, they do it here.

Perhaps your teacher is still thinking of a poem as a physical object—as art collectors think of a painting. A poem is more like a wave on a flow of growth inside a person, and it passes through all of us in this way.

Do you ever rewrite a poem once you have written it?

I wanted to write Miltonic sonnets and I tried very hard to do that for a solid year, so I have done a lot of failed work. I mentioned that I had written for eight years at the start, failing totally because I was trying to write poetry with my right side. Then when the poems of *Silence in the Snowy Fields* came, I set them down with very little rewriting, maybe one or two lines only. Most of them were written outdoors and they arrived complete as they came on whatever little piece of paper I had with me. And there are other poems that I've worked on for ten years.

You were talking about the isolation that you feel is necessary. What I'm interested in finding out is what you think about the poets who go to New York City, or areas that are centers of culture. Did you find that environment was negative?

At certain times there are centers of culture. Paris apparently was like that in the twenties. It's not like that anymore. As the revolution of the printed word goes on, the culture begins to drain out of the centers and the cities begin to die from inside.

I came to New York in 1951, and I was here until 1954. There weren't any communes, I didn't know anybody, but I had a great ecstatic feeling from New York. The intensity of the city helped me a great deal since I came from a very low-energy farm area in Minnesota. I gained nothing from New York as far as conversation with poets was concerned; I didn't meet any.

But now it's quite the reverse of the twenties, the poets who have come to New York and live near a center, like some near St. Marks, have, many of them, evaporated. Perhaps that's because they want the wrong things from a city—what it can't provide. I don't know. Or perhaps there's too much sociability. Many people are living on the land in New Mexico and Oregon, and in the Sierras. San Francisco has some energy. I love to be in San Francisco, but there's still the same problem; there's no center of population that can give you what centers used to give. Thoreau already felt it happening, so he pulled out of Concord. We have to go by ourselves now.

Don't you think that's good though? That now there is more of an opportunity? In other words, I feel I can be wherever I am and do what I have to do.

Yes, I think so too. I was talking with Gary Snyder about it and his sense is that the Age of the Guru is ending. I don't know about that. But he feels that the serious American student now has enough interior intuitional guidance that if he goes by himself and trusts himself or herself, he will make progress without outside "leadership."

As long as there are great paperbacks everywhere and there are great poets writing, it's possible for the solitary student to find psychic guidance moving just a little ahead of his own development. You don't need any place like New York. What you need is a place to work, where you can become transparent, and the unconscious inside you can come forward soberly and guide your growth. I'll read you a poem by Kabir:

> Friend, hope for the Guest while you are alive.
> Jump into experience while you are alive!
> Think . . . and think . . . while you are alive.
> What you call "salvation" belongs to the time before death.

If you don't break your ropes while you're alive,
do you think
ghosts will do it after?

The notion that the soul will join with the ecstatic just
    because
the body is rotten—
that is all fantasy.
What is found now is found then.

If you find nothing now,
you will simply end up with an apartment in the City of
    Death.
If you make love with the Divine now,
in the next life you will have the face of satisfied desire.

So plunge into the truth, find out who the Teacher is,
believe in the Great Sound!

Kabir says, when the Guest is being searched for,
it is the intensity of the longing for the Guest that does all
    the work.
Look at me, and you will see a slave of that intensity.

Kabir didn't go along with orthodox Moslemism, Hin-
duism, or anything else. He says, you want to find it?
Intensity will do the work. Put yourself in a position
where you can be intense. You can be intense when
you're alone, or with a person that you truly love, really,
really love.

Infantilism and Adult Swiftness

An Interview with Ekbert Faas

New York, November, 1974

I

To what degree do you acknowledge Philip Lamantia and David Gascoyne as predecessors for your own attempts to introduce surrealism into Anglo-American poetry?

My view of surrealism came entirely from Spanish and South American surrealism.

It seems to me that in your earlier poetry collected in Silence in the Snowy Fields *you are influenced by D. H. Lawrence.*

No. *Silence in the Snowy Fields* looks back to Synge; and a couple of translations that Frank O'Connor made of medieval Irish work which moved me greatly; and then there is Antonio Machado. He is the father of that book.

And you hadn't read D. H. Lawrence at all at the time?

I had read a few poems, but among the English Wordsworth is a much deeper influence.

But then there is all that imagery of going into the depths, into the dark, and into the sea of death, etc., which seems exactly like in Lawrence.

No link. I never read much of D. H. Lawrence's poetry until someone gave me the three-volume edition four or five years later. The only one I knew well is "Bavarian Gentians" which I think is a great great great great poem.

That's the poem I was thinking of, actually.

I still learn much from Lawrence, not from his poetry, but from the motion that he made away from the intellect and down into the body.

So you do respect him.

Oh tremendously. The essay in the middle of *Sleepers Joining Hands* is full of mad generalizations for which I first saw the possibility in *Fantasia of the Unconscious.* Why not? A book of unsupportable generalizations about things that interest us. I don't think my essay would exist without *Fantasia of the Unconscious.*

There is an interesting book about surrealism by Ulrich Kellerer who claims that Western art, after a transitional period of surrealism, or after crossing the "dark psychic woods of the unconscious," as you would call it, is moving closer and closer to a Zen Buddhist approach to reality. Does that kind of general overview make sense to you? Kellerer describes Pollock as approaching Eastern calligraphic painting techniques, for instance.

We could imagine a poetry in which a great "flowing" consciousness is present, and the outer world is also present. In ancient Buddhist art the world is very very very very present. The artist is aware of it all the time. Such an artist would never do as Pollock does and scatter it around like this, because in doing so he has dissolved the world, he has returned to the state of the infant in which the world is not clear. I respect Pollock a great deal, but I would think he is the *end* of a Western tradition and that he has nothing to do with the calligraphers, because the calligraphers are dealing with content. When they are doing a calligraphy, every one of their curves to them has the shape of a mountain or a moon in mist.

And you don't think that the impulse of action painting could finally incorporate that concreteness?

I don't know. The tendency now is for everything in art to break the link with the adult energy of the unconscious, if you can say such a thing, and instead to proceed back toward the crib. The baby is also spontaneous. So you have two movements here, which appear alike, but are not. There is a very interesting book entitled *Man-Child: A Study of the Infantilization of Man,* by David Jonas and Doris Klein. It is an impressive book. If the infantilism continues, all the things Lawrence stood for will be destroyed. I've just translated a poem by H. Martinson about D. H. Lawrence:

You waited for the hour when all things would take on soul
    again,
and taste, feeling, and soul would touch them,
as the day of inwardness came.

But the world was extroverted.
Only misunderstanding really thrived.

The new deep communion you sang of did not happen.
The interior table was set,
But only a few came
and only a few of those were capable of eating.
The rest came out of a meaningless curiosity.

The church in the body had to be locked up.
Now it stands open to the storm of steel, given over
to the demons of extroversion.

It's a good poem, and it gives another way to understand Pop Art. Pop Art makes sense to me in terms of infantilization. The sense of adulthood is weak with us; it is stronger in the European psyche, and even more so in the Chinese. They imagine adulthood as the ability to balance yin and yang.

Let's return to surrealism and open form. Both are launch points into the unknown. We launch out, and go away from patriarchal form, and then what happens? There is a powerful magnet over there, not far away, near the wall. It is the magnet of the crib, or the cradle, or "the primitive man." It is too strong in America; it's too strong! It pulls art down into the crib; it pulls it backward. The New York school of recent years in art and poetry has not gone forward into the union of yang and yin as the ancient Chinese art and poetry did. Chinese artists moved for a thousand years into adult minglings of yin and yang, of mist and discipline. We go a little way away from the patriarchal and start to curve down. The lethargy in the colleges is a form of infantilism.

You once said that "the road to the new brain goes through the forest." That, in a way, seems to summarize what you have been talking about right now.

Yes, following that imagery, what we do is we find a

gingerbread house in the forest and stay there. We never bother to put the witch into her own oven. We just ask for more cookies.

The Sufis and the Buddhists leave the gingerbread house and aim for an adult consciousness. But in order to reach that, the soul has to go through the mammal brain, which means it has to go into human suffering and into the body, into a deep sexual life. Lawrence says a man, like a flower, is "fertilized" by a strong sexual experience.

As Americans, we have to go through the mammal brain, but we don't want to do that. We went into the Vietnam war and did all that reptile killing and we now refuse to go through the mammal grief. I ended the reading last night with poems of Kabir, and the students' faces lit up all over the room. It was beautiful. That ecstasy is what they want more than anything, but they don't want to go through the grief of the mammal brain in order to get there.

Of course, that's an impression that one frequently gets in America, that people think they can take a shortcut to the new consciousness.

And one has to say in favor of Ted Hughes that he goes through the mammal, though he may not arrive at the new brain. The new brain is not so prominent in him. As Marie Louise von Franz would say, he is a little "caught" by black magic, and black magic hates the new brain. He's a little "caught" there. That's expressed by the crow, which is black. He wants someone to take him and bring him out, someone to bring him out of that. But there is nobody that's that far in, so nobody can help him. I see him as a suffering mammal, a great suffering mammal.

Are there any contemporary artists whose work parallels what you are trying to achieve in poetry?

I feel a strong kinship with Morris Graves, Max Ernst, de Kooning, Jean Arp and with some work of Rauschenberg. To me Max Ernst is great, inexhaustible. I don't know any recent surrealist poetry that comes near his *Une Semaine de Bonté.*

But isn't that still deep "in the forest"?

Certainly, oh yes.

But do you see any glimpses of light from the open country on the other side?

There is something luminous about his paintings; the open country is floating all through them. The open country lives in Jean Arp's sculpture also.

But I was thinking of more recent art.

Well, Rauschenberg, I think, is a genius—sometimes!

But how about your criticism of Pop Art?

Rauschenberg is not only a Pop Artist.

I remember you saying that Pop Art—in Lawrence's terms—is putting the umbrella up again where surrealism had taken it down.

Did I? Lawrence said that when you look up, in most centuries, you do not see the black sky with stars, but instead an opened umbrella on which artists have painted some stars. Humanity prefers that, it is less scary. A strong artist will tear holes in the umbrella so you can see the stars again. Eliot did that, so did the surrealists. The whole Andy Warhol school is just putting the umbrella up again. I like Lawrence's image—it explains a lot to me. None of Warhol's movies tear open anything, just as pornography never tears open anything, it closes instead. The point of commercial pornography is to prevent you from experiencing. This is only my opinion; most people don't agree with me.

No, I wouldn't either.

Most people think Andy Warhol is part of the avant-garde, I don't.

To me, your poetic development shows a curious reversal of the development we talked about in relation to Kellerer's book. In this way Silence in the Snowy Fields *seems to have been written, not by a man "deep in the forest" of the unconscious, but by one who has traversed that forest and has come out on the other side. You have often referred to a period of depression, solitude, and self-analysis, in New York, I gather, before you began to write poetry, and I wondered how that period relates to your first collection of poetry and what kind of experiences you went through during that period.*

I'd rather not talk about that very much. But you're right in your sense of the order. I did write some surrealism before *Silence in the Snowy Fields.* I didn't put it in because I didn't want to break the tone of *Silence.*

So biographically speaking your development doesn't

really reverse the general historical one in which surrealism seems to precede the kind of consciousness which *must have inspired* Silence in the Snowy Fields.

But then there is no reason that surrealism cannot return later. At any point it may be necessary for you to return to the confusion of the unconscious again.

But you don't want to talk about that period in New York.

I describe it in the autobiographical poem in *Sleepers Joining Hands* as well as I can. I was simply living in a small room, very poor. [Pause.] Anyway it wasn't a period in which I did much writing. I understood Sartre's *Nausea* very well in those days. I didn't care for Sartre at all until I had been there for about two years, until I picked it up. I read the first five pages and I felt weak, almost fainted.

Most American poets seem to bypass the crisis described in Nausea, *I mean the whole consciousness and language crisis which had such a devastating effect on many European poets—actually destroyed them as poets. Like Hugo von Hofmannsthal, for instance, who was probably the first to undergo that experience. He wrote all his greatest poetry before he turned twenty-four, then suffered the crisis he describes in his famous "Lord Chandos Letter" [1902], and after that just stopped writing poetry. Of course, what Gary Snyder says concerning this whole problem makes sense to me: that a poet like Hofmannsthal really wanted to be some kind of philosopher-magus. Paradoxically, it was Wittgenstein who turned Gary himself to poetry.*

That language crisis involves the emotion of disgust. "You are defiled by what comes out of your mouth."

That's like the phrase Hofmannsthal uses in the "Lord Chandos Letter": that words seemed to disintegrate in his mouth like mouldering mushrooms.

What I'd like to discuss is your concept of the image.

I'm not fond of the term "deep image."

Yes, I noticed that you avoid it in your criticism. But you have never given a detailed description or definition of what you mean by image.

Let's try to make a distinction between "projection" and "image." Pound and Eliot both believed that a feeling is best kept fresh in art by being "projected" onto the outer world. "Smells of steaks in passageways" becomes an objective correlative of a certain feeling of mingled fatigue and despair Eliot experienced when he entered rooming houses. The substances "smells" "steaks" and "passageways" can all be taken out of the work of art and reinserted back into the world. So they are "objective." Eliot doesn't use projection exclusively, he uses it mostly. Then, if "smells of steaks in passageways" is a projection of an inner fatigue out onto objects, what is an "image"? I'll quote some lines of Lorca, and then of Trakl:

> I want to sleep for half a second,
> a second, a minute, a century,
> but I want everyone to know that I'm still alive,
> that I am the little friend of the west wind,
> that I am the elephantine shadow of my own tears.

Somehow the psychic energy has remained inside the

psyche, and there it created a new substance, "the elephantine shadow of my own tears."

Trakl says:

> On silver soles I climbed down the thorny stairs, and I walked into the white-washed room. A light burned there silently, and without speaking I wrapped my head in purple linen; and the earth threw out a child's body, a creature of the moon, that slowly stepped out of the darkness of my shadow, and with broken arms dropped over a stony waterfall, fluffy snow.

You notice that the psyche is in a state of great energy. Moving with its own immense energy, it becomes equal to the world. Instead of depending on the outer world for support, it begins somehow to create a third world, neither "physical" nor "inner."

It's as if a human being and a badger together would give birth to an angel. Or as if an angel and a tree gave birth to a bridge. It's as if a bull woke up one day with so much energy, he ignored the fence posts and barn door of his pasture and created Assyria instead!!

We're so used to "fence-post and barn-door poetry" we don't recognize what Lorca is doing. We all write barn-door poetry. Most political poetry is barn-door poetry, and most love poetry now.

The phrase "deep image" suggests a geographical location in the psyche. It misses what the bull does. So I didn't feel that Robert Kelly caught the physicalness of the image in his "Deep Image" essay. Kelly has a wonderfully strong mind, but it's not especially physical. Rothenberg's mind is more physical.

I spent a day with Rothenberg several months ago, and liked him.

He and I were friends, and still are, and we had conversations and planned magazines in which we tried to bring forward ideas of this sort. He did *Poems of the Floating World.*

Let me quote a few phrases by Duncan who says that the image should be "close to the psychological archetype of Jungian analysis" or that it should be an "evocation of depth . . . not unrelated to the neo-Platonic images." Also he says that the image should be a "received sign of the great language in which the universe itself is written."

I like the last one best. I get sick of hearing Plato's name spoken in every discussion of the image. I agree an image can be "close" to an archetype, but the way to ruin a poem is to put in a lot of archetypes. I insist the image is a physical thing, and Plato doesn't know a thing about that.

We don't have to work on this [pointing to his brain]. We become successful through *this,* but the mysterious thing is that art is created with this [pointing to his heart]. What was the last one again?

The image is a "received sign of the great language in which the universe itself is written," which is really an Orphic concept.

And Orpheus, as you know, decided to go down here [pointing to his body].

The first one makes most sense to me.

They all make "sense," but it's a question of tone.

So you would hesitate to formulate a phrase or definition like that.

I would try to avoid it.

*Like associating the image with Jungian archetypes and
so forth.*

I hate the word archetype.

*Can you make any statement as to how images originate
in your consciousness?*

No.

Why not?

I don't *want* to make any statements on that. If I do, in
this rapid tone, I'd make it with my thinking function.
It wouldn't be just to the experience to describe it with
one-fourth of the brain!

*Did you know that Duncan has criticized imagism in
almost the exact same terms you use?*

I'm not surprised.

*How does your admiration for Chinese poetry relate to
all this? After all, there don't seem to be many images
like "death in the deep roads of the guitar" in Chinese
poetry.*

On the contrary, there are lots, and we can't get them
through the English language, because the translators are
used to "projection" poetry and they translate the poems
into the barn-door poetry they know. Until Trakl's and
Lorca's true image poetry penetrates into the minds of
the scholars who translate Chinese, until that happens,

we will be blind to Chinese poetry. In the meantime we have A. C. Graham's translations of *Poems of the Late T'ang.* In Li Ho you'll see images almost too wild to be disguised.

So you would say that there is a very strong element in Far Eastern poetry of what in Western terminology we'd call surrealist imagery?

Oh yes, very strong. Another way of talking about their sophistication would be to talk of the union of the senses. Here is a little poem of Basho's. He is listening to the temple bells in his garden.

> The temple bell stops,
> But the sound keeps coming
> Out of the flowers.

Basho has taken a sound and changed it into an odor. That's something that an imagist couldn't do, or at least has not, to my knowledge, done. This art belongs to the whole area of changing of substances and transforming them. The ancient Chinese and Japanese poetry is far ahead of ours. American students in the poetry workshops have a hard time bringing an odor in its natural form into a poem, so we smell it as an odor. It's rare to hear a sound that's not a language sound in an American poem! It's rare to see green in a poem! Imagine being so at home in them that you could transform them!

II

How do you relate to Breton's concept of automatic writing? Do you think it's a useful exercise.

No.

My feeling is that exercises in automatic writing, even if they wouldn't have produced the actual poetry, could have had a very liberating effect on Hart Crane, for instance.

Automatic writing to me has more to do with Freud than with poetry.

That's more or less how T. S. Eliot felt about it, although he had to admit that parts of The Waste Land *were composed in an efflux of poetry approaching the condition of automatic writing.*

That's probably why it doesn't hold together as a work of art. Automatic writing evidently comes from fragmented parts of the psyche; and they are not connected to the whole and they are just like men at the edges of the raft crying, trying to make one realize that they're out there; and he brought too many of them into *The Waste Land*; the result is that it falls apart as a work of art. Its victory was a human victory, of compassion and listening.

Of course, later he became almost ashamed of his poem, calling it a mere piece of rhythmical grumbling.

That's so typical. What he's gone through he feels obliged to deny to others. But there are real images in *The Waste Land,* "bats with baby faces in the violet light / Whistled, and beat their wings / And crawled head downward down a blackened wall." Bats with baby faces in the violet light cannot be inserted into the universe or taken away. They are something insane, from another world.

At the beginning of my essay I compare these lines with some of your own.

I'd like to see it. I love that passage, love it, love it. "A woman drew her long black hair out tight / And fiddled whisper music on those strings."

I'd like to come back to your concept of creativity for a moment. In my studies of Chinese aesthetics I found that the ancient literati talk endlessly about painting techniques but rarely about poetic creativity.

It's not really worth investigating maybe; it would be different for every poet.

Whereas the painter calligraphists seem to be talking about the same thing most of the time: a kind of gestural automatism, a complete fusion with the subject matter, etc.

Lovely, but I don't think we are advanced enough to do that.

I wondered if there might be any analogue to that in poetic creativity.

Probably.

And I thought it was Olson's great contribution to have rediscovered this physiological basis of poetic creativity, this genuine spontaneity in contrast to the fictitious spontaneity of Romantic nature poetry.

On the other hand there are no real objects in Olson's poetry; perceived without the intrusion of the intellect or the ego.

That's exactly what he criticized in Pound.

It's a problem with intuitive types. There are no cows; a cow is a symbol for some part of his psyche. There are no horses; every horse is a symbol of part of his psyche. In a way, Jung is like that.

And surrealism would avoid that, in your opinion.

Although in *most* surrealism the author is again using only the intuitive part of his intelligence. It's possible that a great work of art cannot come out through using only one of our "functions" or "intelligences." It's as mistaken as Yvor Winters trying to use only his thinking function. In good Spanish or South American surrealism the world is often present, as well as the inner impulses from the unconscious. I'm not sure where Breton is in this. I don't feel "the world" so much in his poems. His younger followers evidently feel that the surrealism is more intense and more daring and more genuine if the world itself is left out. That is one reason they hate Neruda. Several American surrealists have written me letters attacking me for translating Neruda. Some surrealists feel also that if the Vietnam war appears in a poem otherwise surrealist, it is a violation of the ideals of surrealism. The Puritan wishes to control the interior of his world, the American surrealist wishes to control the interior of *his* world. Neruda is wise to call for "impure poetry." I think a surrealist who tries to shut off in his own poems political comment is involved in Puritanism. Of course, he sees his point of view as wildly anti-Puritanical. But we all have many surprises for each other.

But is there any principle as to how you make images interconnect?

There, you are doing it again. I don't *make* the images interconnect. If they don't and I notice it, I throw the poem away.

And how do you notice it?

Reading the poem.

So again you wouldn't like to make an analytical statement about that?

No.

In an interview from the year 1972 you stated that the thinking which in the last eight or nine years you have learned most from has been Buddhist and I wondered if Buddhism has also influenced your writing and creativity.

You are asking questions in a pre-Lawrence way, you are trying to fragment the psyche too much, and you are forcing me to think of myself as a third person. It's wrong to try and pin down religious influence. Perhaps an intelligent theory of meter could be discussed. But Buddhism, if it has influence, influences the entire psyche, it has to do with the integration of previously disconnected parts of the psyche, therefore you can't point to any one thing.

I was mainly thinking of my own comparison between action painting and Chinese calligraphy, that in both cases the artist abandons himself to the autonomous movements of his body.

Buddhism doesn't do that, Buddhism is very disciplined, they hate that kind of stuff.

I would speak of disciplined spontaneity.

Mu Ch'i made an ink wash of five pears. They are done with ink, I take it, and so could not be corrected. I suppose it took maybe thirty-five seconds.

Quite.

But this is preceded by fifteen years of this discipline. In the West we want to have "autonomous movement of the limbs" before the fifteen years are over.

I couldn't agree more. One can see some of that disciplined spontaneity in the work of Peter Brook and Jerzy Grotowski when compared with most Happenings.

Happenings belong to the history of infantilism in my opinion. I repeat that I feel a danger in your questions, namely that you are drawn to the work of Lawrence and after, but approach it in a pre-Lawrence way.

But how does one avoid that?

How would Lawrence ask a question?

But you know, I'm not Lawrence. I'm just a university trained European intellectual. [Both laughing.]

Oh, now don't give me that modesty stuff!

I'm not really trying to be evasive. I know the shortcomings of what I'm doing or rather of the way I'm doing it only too well.

I don't mean shortcomings. I mean that you have a responsibility to Lawrence if he is one of your heroes. He says it is important to approach a problem from the point of view of the whole psyche. He opposes his new approach to the old fragmented or intellectualist approach. You're asking me for intellectualist formulations of various experiences which are bound to fragment the experience. I like your intellectual energy. But you might try to ask the questions in a Lawrence or post-Lawrence way. You might have to interpret the answer. I don't know what it would be like. But I sense it's harmful to your own psyche to ask intellectualist questions.

As a motto for one of your books you use those beautiful lines by Basho:

> The morning glory—
> another thing
> that will never by my friend.

I think that's an example of what one can learn from Zen Buddhism or Eastern philosophy generally.

I agree.

III

In one of his interviews, Ginsberg explains how the gaps between his images make the concrete world of the poem transparent for the final emptiness of the Absolute, the "blissful empty void" or sunyata, *as the Buddhists call it. Does that notion make sense to you?*

What makes me vomit is that last thing, the "blissful empty void" or *sunyata*. We are all tourists of the East, all Westerners are, and we take their concepts and we misuse them constantly because of our crude psychological development. I've done it many times myself, I'm sure, I misuse them crudely, but somewhere there's a line which one shouldn't pass, and *sunyata* is an extremely serious concept or state. I think no Westerner has ever experienced it except perhaps San Juan de la Cruz or Santa Teresa de Avila. Now to have this dragged over and stuck into a little passage about poetry is revolting. I feel the same way about the phrase "Dharma Bums," can't stand it. It's exploitation not different from what the American soldier did in Vietnam, and Ginsberg doesn't realize in my opinion that when he uses a phrase like this he is violating the Buddhist religion in the same way that American marines violated a village.

Would the same apply to Gary Snyder as well, in your opinion?

No, no. Once in a while, maybe. It applies to me too once in a while. But Gary has worked on the problem, he has worked hard, very hard. And these concepts need to be brought in, they are very valuable, but somehow the concepts are being destroyed. The poet's job is to keep language fresh, and Ginsberg is aware of that. And yet he takes a word like *sunyata* and throws it in any old place; he's cheapening language. Why does he do that?

You've often attacked Ginsberg.

I don't attack him.

At least there are various critical remarks throughout your prose writings. You spoke of his "lack of gentleness."

Where did I say that?

Somewhere in The Sixties, *I think I could find it for you.*

Ginsberg's lack of gentleness?

Yes. Then you criticize him for his use of four letter words and shocking subjects.

That must have been in 1958, in *The Fifties,* number 1.

And then you accused him for giving up "all hope of imaginative precision and delicacy."

When was that?

I don't have the exact reference here, but somewhere in The Sixties, *I think. I could quote a lot more.* [Both laughing.]

That's interesting.

But recently you have called him the "clear rebirth . . . of a very powerful spiritual man" and have approvingly quoted his remark that "as soon as you have a new syntax, you have a new way of breathing and as soon as you have that you have a new consciousness." Has there been any change in your attitude toward Ginsberg?

There has. I wrote an article for the *American Poetry Review* recently giving examples in poetry of the "four intelligences" Jung talks about. They are thinking, feeling, grasp of the senses, and intuition. I gave Louis Simpson as an example of a thinking man basically. I mentioned

that the hostility early on that thinking types felt to-
ward Ginsberg was connected with the perception that he
was urging them to develop their weak feeling function.
I think that's true of my early hositility to Ginsberg.

So you're really saying your peccavi here.

Yes, of course.

But at the same time we all notice that Ginsberg's
spiritual gift is mingled with some sort of sloppy lan-
guage. I mentioned that earlier. You see the problem. I
feel two people in him. One is spiritual, one not. Re-
cently I have been able to separate those two more. One
part of Allen urges you on to develop your feeling areas,
and since feeling is open on one side to the spirit, he
is actually urging you to develop spirit. Then there's
another being in him urging you to remain content with
clutter. I'm thinking of the poem in his new book from
a meditation retreat in Colorado describing his breath
going out over the country to Lowell, Massachusetts,
then to Kyoto, Vietnam, etc. It is a sort of tourist poem,
with a couple of anecdotes of each place. The poem
loads us down with memory clutter, so the poem some-
how misrepresents meditation. One half of him is the
grandmother, and the other half is the wolf! But the
grandmother is so amazingly generous. It comes out in
his singing, too.

So you have become friends.

Oh yes. Yes. We read together whenever we can. Once in
my house, he saw a group of anthologies in a bookcase,
and said, "Well, Robert, when we're both in all those
anthologies, then what?" That's how wise the grand-
mother is.

[I next read Bly the passage from the essay dealing with his 1967 attack on James Dickey. This lead to a long and fascinating discussion of "The Firebombing" and "Slave Quarters" which Bly, however, preferred to delete from the typescript manuscript of the interview, saying there is too much criticism of others here.—E. Faas]

IV

In your criticism you have mainly drawn attention to the poetries outside the Anglo-American tradition. Occasionally, but not very often, you mention Wordsworth whom you compare with the Chinese poet Tao Yuan Ming, or Yeats as having the sense of "Gott-Natur," or Blake who took a first step into the psychic forest. Are there any other English or American poets with whom you feel a deep affinity?

Besides Yeats and Blake—Chaucer, certainly. Even more the Grail poets, the Tristan poet, and the author of *Gawain and the Green Knight*. To me they are most contemporary.

Duncan and before him Pound have argued that it was during the period of the romances that the Western mind, for a short phase at least, began to recuperate some of the energy and imagery repressed by Christianity.

I'm just beginning to think of the possibility of the Grail poems being reworkings of Sufi literature. I have instead seen them as vigorous attempts to bring forward the feminine in man, in the male. Shortly after the Grail work, the movement was entirely crushed. The church moves in after the fourteenth century A.D. Respect for the feminine doesn't rise again until the Romantic age, but it appears once more in our time. Pound touched on Troubadour poetry, but Pound doesn't seem involved in the spirit—or the link between the spirit and the feminine.

What the Grail poems discuss even more is some strange creature who is wounded. He has a bit of steel or iron in his testicles, and he can't be healed; this wound remains unhealed century after century. So there is such a thing as "wound literature." It is ignored through the whole eighteenth century. The European psyche knows it is wounded. It's a profound wound which will not heal, and in the eighteenth century people did not discuss it. They put a plaster or a bandage over it. In the nineteenth century, writers live out the agony of the wound. But they still will not investigate it, and it's only in our time that the wound is beginning to live and be lived again— also in words—

The Waste Land *brings it up.*

I think so.

Ted Hughes once described the poem to me as a love poem for this degraded and desecrated female spirit.

He's right surely. [Pause.] Aristotle caused a wound and the Grail legends talk about that wound, now no work is of any value that does not face the wound. . . .

You take Aristotle as being representative of Hellenistic rationalism, I guess.

That kind of thing, yes. The Middle Ages centered around Aristotle, the whole mentality that led to the Ph.D. as well as to secularism. And I personally think that the Aristotle mentality is related to the mass-man also. Ortega y Gasset's *Revolt of the Masses*—what a powerful book! Underneath, Aquinas and Aristotle are much alike. One is the religious version, the other the secular version. The Grail legends describe the wound made by the Catholic church that foolishly adopted Aristotle.

Ernst Topitsch has described how this fusion of Hellenistic and Christian thought leads right up to Hegel and Marx. . . .

. . . and leaves out an entire world, which is the world hinted at in the "romances." They are still secret literature, secret literature for a small group.

Duncan links that to Gnosticism, neo-Platonism, Hermeticism, and all the other heretical movements. . . .

Yes. Bosch also. Centuries later Dürer appears with his great femininity, his combination of femininity and precision; in the twentieth century Antonio Machado. In between the two there is Blake. Blake talks about the wound in "Oh Rose thou art sick."

So you feel that Romanticism initiated Modernism.

I do surely.

V

Do you feel that American poets of the last two decades

have responded to your plea, made in the late fifties, that they must traverse the dark psychic woods of the unconscious before they will be able to write a truly great modern poetry?

I don't believe that it's possible to write post-Lawrentian poetry, or "wound poetry," or however you want to describe it, without solitude; and when people in the universities try to write such poetry they often find the style without the way of life; it sends them off on just another sidetrack. I think that's what's happening. The style has been picked up but I don't see much deep change. I underestimated how much a style is a part of a way of life. Rilke is right at the end of his Apollo poem where he says that to write differently you have to change your *life.*

You have often criticized Olson for embodying the "formalist obsession" of American poetry. On the other hand I find that your own position is not at all antagonistic to Olson's. I see it as complementary . . .

Sure, why not.

. . . rather than antagonistic to him. But why then did you have to attack him for something which is not even at the center of his poetics. I mean there is so much more to Olson than his concern with breath rhythm, prosody, and so forth. For instance, his concern with the physiological autonomy of the creative process.

Several times—maybe those remarks are in interviews or essays you haven't seen—I've said about Olson that I respect his intellectual speculations tremendously.

I started my magazine to clear ground for myself and for other poets. By 1964 the ground was absolutely and entirely covered with Charles Olson bushes. There was not a spot of ground that was not shaded by a Charles Olson bush. Creeley after a long correspondence with Charles Olson formulated the dogma "form is never more than an extension of content." Olson praised it, and most writers since find it self-evident. But I don't think the statement is true at all.

I have the feeling that I sense Bach's mathematical form with one part of myself, and his ecstatic freedom with another part. That implies there are two separate forces meeting in a third body.

Field published a weird essay recently by Donald Hall, in which he suggested that some of the oral or breast sensuality of infancy goes into sound in poetry, and so into form. He suspects that poetic form is linked with archaic layers of the pleasure instinct, experienced first with depth in infancy. I add that some of the adult grasp of "the world" goes into content. We can see that such a visualization is incompatible with the accepted idea Olson has praised. Far from form and content being extensions, one of the other, it is more likely they are distinct and opposite forces, opposite in charge.

I wrote a letter to *Field* commenting on this issue, and I'll read you a couple of paragraphs:

Charles Olson wonderfully understood that American poetic form could not be an imitation of English form, and that the roots of form go back to the body and its breath, not to English metrical habits. It seems though that he wanted the form to be adult—he was interested in the time after the invention of the typewriter, rather than the primitive time before the baby or the aborigine has ever seen a typewriter.

His essay on projective verse makes the whole problem of

form technical, post-industrial, needing ingenuity and a typewriter with a good spacer. I'm unjust to his intellectual liveliness, but there is some Puritanism, that is, dislike of childhood, in his essay. Russian poets don't seem to have that.

Even Duncan would agree with that, I think.

Suppose a work of art is a container of energy, a sort of battery, then bland formulations of the unity of form and content merely mislead young poets as to what a work of art is. There something bland in much Black Mountain poetry.

You know, that at the Berkeley reading, being obviously quite drunk and stoned, he said that he was really in love with Our Lady of Christ.

I think he must have been a lively man. As a person, as a teacher, he was evidently extremely warm, with a fantastically big mammal brain. He taught Creeley an amazing number of things. But to go back, suppose we use open form. The question is how do you bring infantile pleasure or Pound sensuality into an open form poem?

Snyder is very concerned with that.

Is he?

Oh yes. How do you get that rhythmic sensuality back into open form poetry?

Sensuality seems the right word to use.

You once said that objectivism—and I don't think that's fair to Olson's objectism—is an evasion of self. I feel that both you and Olson are rather more interested in a kind of self-transcendence.

Yes, yes.

You achieve it by delving into the unconscious, whereas Olson achieves it by trying to abandon himself to some kind of automatous, automatic process of creativity akin to what Werner Haftmann calls the gestural expressionism of action painting—a physiological process which is larger than himself and in which he fuses with the flux of nature.

Absolutely right.

So I don't understand why you object. . . .

When he says that we must try to avoid "the soul getting between us and the objects," I agree, and yet, what does it mean? It's a secular statement, an Aristotelian statement. So therefore I find him coming from two sides; he makes Aristotelian statements and yet he struggles against the Aristotelian box. By an Aristotelian I mean someone who encourages a naked confrontation between "mind" and "object," with the "soul" left out. That's vague, I know. But it's possible we *share* soul with objects. How could we then leave out soul as we try to get near objects? It's possible we're not the only beings who *have* soul!

I do like the way he thinks from scratch. "I go down and look at the Mayan tombs and no one has ever looked at them with a fresh eye as I have." Pound looked at economics that way. The American apparently longs to be the amateur discoverer. It's a great weakness and a great strength. I do it too. I try to throw off the European mind background, and then I have to become an amateur psychologist if not an amateur archaeologist. You understand that impulse? It's very American, very American. It's all through Hemingway. Hemingway says: "The Europeans don't know anything about style. I found a style. I found it in the woods." That impulse is in all of us.

Talking about the form of a poem you once spoke of its "mysterious arbitrariness." You also said that it is obsolete to consider form as the most important thing about a poem. And, finally in a statement reminiscent of Pound and Lawrence, you said that a great work of art often has at its center "a long floating leap around which the work gathers like steel shavings around a magnet."

Magnetic energy gives so many possibilities for understanding art. In the leaping sentence I'm thinking of content. The substance of a poem arranges itself round the center leap. In the *Odyssey* the poem first leaps into the Great Mother, and then all the scenes such as visiting Circe, visiting the Cyclops, going down to the dead, center themselves naturally around the initial leap. The poem takes its form that way without mind intervention.

Creeley claims that he usually writes a poem in one stretch, so that the order in which the words appear on the page reflects exactly the chronological sequence of creativity. Or Snyder told me that he often completes a poem in his mind and then just transcribes it onto the page. By contrast you once said that you wrote about ten thousand lines for the poem called "Sleepers Joining Hands" and only published about four hundred. Do you revise just by throwing things away like Creeley while leaving the rest untouched?

I revise by magnetics, see what holds on. In that poem, I didn't know what the poem was about so I worked in confusion for four years.

In a totally open process of creative discovery.

Evidently, that's why I wrote so many lines.

Of course, Snyder, likewise, uses a totally different way of writing in composing the various sections of Mountains and Rivers without End.

Yes. There must be other ways, too.

VI

Last night you spoke of three levels of consciousness. In the lowest level there is a great deal of repression, violence, and isolation. On the second level the man or woman—you gave D. H. Lawrence as an example—moves out past his ego into creatures and trees. Then you read Kabir's ecstatic poems as an example of work on the third level. How does "open form" relate to these three levels?

I haven't though this over myself.

Let's say first that writing a good rhymed and metered poem means that the man or woman has learned how to repress successfully. Repressing well is a valuable art in civilization, as important as knowing how to build with wood. We repress constantly. When Breton, for example, allows angry lobsters with hair to come up, at the same second he is repressing tenderness. The problem is that when we're young, we don't choose what to repress. We repress firmly, but not wisely. In other words the material stays down. Poets who write a great deal of rhymed verse in their twenties have trouble growing, because their literary self-respect becomes associated with successful repression. We all know examples of that. Frost is one, on a wide scale.

Let's try to relate that idea to states of consciousness. The man or woman in the lowest stage—where we are most of the day—experiences constant projection. The American man is not angry, other people are. He is not feminine, Marilyn Monroe is. The American woman says: "I am not dark inside, the blacks are dark." She is not obsessed with force, the Russians are obsessed with force. But the marvelous discovery Freud and Jung made is that only energies already pushed out of sight are projected onto others' faces. We can't get hold of our energies, only see them on the faces of others. As a man, I can't get hold of my female side, I can only see it on the faces of women. This inability to get hold of our energies is an experience in the lowest stage of consciousness. We have all had those experiences thousands of times.

To return then to rhymed and metered poems. . . . The poet says, "I am not orderly inside, the poem is." This projection, like all projection, is dangerous when it becomes a habit. Frost's life got more and more disorderly as that *habit* took hold.

"Free verse" or "open form" then is not a literary technique—that's why I dislike Olson's essay "Projective Verse"—that's odd—projective verse!—but it is a step in growth. It is a way to encourage us to let up a little in repression, ease up the projection, and move out a bit from the lowest stage of consciousness. It doesn't always succeed, and those who write rhymed and metered poetry today don't always stay in the lowest stage of consciousness, by any means. We're dealing in tendencies, possibilities, only. Richard Wilbur did not stay there.

As a person moves from the first to the second level of consciousness, he or she allows some repressed material to rise—just as you are allowing it to rise in your hallucinations.

That's right.

Here's a possible visualization of it, that I see. Each time we enter the second level there may be three sudden movements taking place at the same instant. Energy pushed down rises up toward you from below; then the brother of that energy sent off to live on the faces of others descends down to you . . . at the same moment your feminine soul appears as a speck on the horizon rushing toward you. If a woman is writing the poem, or experiencing the second stage, the movements are identical except that her masculine soul is what appears far away hurrying toward her. There is a lot of swift and vigorous motion, as of dancing, involved.

What "open form" and Lawrence's "we have come through" and Marianne Moore's intuitive joinings of disparate material without "classical form" and Neruda's jumble in the *Residencia* poems mean is not that repression is bad, but that we need a different cycle of repression and release than we have had.

From what I've said about release, we can guess what the third stage would be like. I suspect the idea of "open form" falls away in the third stage—the man's feminine side would be close to him, I think, and he would feel light for the first time. The woman's male side would be close to her—as the male side of Marie Louise von Franz has come very close to her. You feel in her prose that she's projecting very little. But some. We cannot enter paradise, we cannot in this life, we cannot have all the exiled material returned. Marie Louise has said that over and over.

You think that some of Gary Snyder's poems reach that stage?

Certainly.

I have that feeling too. Do you identify the new brain with this third level?

No, not really when I come to think of it—I don't think so. I would guess we need all our brains at that stage.

I was a bit puzzled that you called Creeley a poet of "the steady light," who tended to remain in one brain when he writes. To me it seems that he is a poet fascinated by "emptiness," like Mallarmé: "The poem supreme, addressed to emptiness."

I don't know how to answer that. He has a weird path of his own. I don't really understand it, but I respect it. I feel very close to him—I kiss him when I see him.

I am going to see him up in Buffalo in a couple of weeks.

Then please tell him from me that I think his new poem about his mother in the hospital is marvelous.

Knots of Wild Energy

An Interview with Wayne Dodd

Athens, Ohio, May, 1978

*I see a curious contradiction in contemporary poetry.
On the one hand, there is the most incredible amount of
poetic activity going on. On the other hand, there is evi-
dence of a real absence of sureness of direction and even
purpose. This uncertainty is reflected even in such things
as a call recently by a literary magazine for people to
comment on what is to be the role of, say, form, or con-
tent, in poetry. It seemed to be symptomatic of a deep
uncertainty. I wonder what would be a way of trying to
make sense of that. Maybe you could talk about, for ex-
ample, what the generation of poets under thirty-five
show us, in their work, that would comment on this.*

I think I feel the same disquiet as you do. Twenty years
ago there may have been fifteen books of poetry pub-
lished every year. Now, there may be sixty or seventy.
They are published by the commercial presses, by the
university presses like Pitt, and maybe another hundred
or two hundred by small presses. I think the directory of
poets includes four or five hundred poets now. It's an ex-
tremely new situation, because poetry in this country has
always been associated with what could be called knots
of wild energy, scattered at different places through-

out the country. In the fifties there were only a few visible: William Carlos Williams, E. E. Cummings, Richard Eberhart, Kenneth Rexroth, Robinson Jeffers, Wallace Stevens, and Marianne Moore. They were geographically separate, and none were connected to universities. Ezra Pound and T. S. Eliot were in Europe. They represented self-creating and self-regulating knots of psychic energy. In fact they resembled wild animals. Even though Wallace Stevens was working for an insurance agency, the part of him that wrote poetry was a wild animal.

It seems to me that what has taken place is the domestication of poetry. If you're going to follow that through, you're going to have to imagine the mink or the otter being brought into cages and bred there. Oftentimes, animals reproduce more in captivity because the young are not killed off. If you bring a species to optimum conditions, you have a vast supply of them in the next generation. But the new otters don't know the same things that their parents did. The original otter knew what cold water was like or knew how to live in the snow. That's one metaphor to explain the amazing tameness of the sixty to eighty volumes of poetry published each year, compared with the compacted energy of a book by Robinson Jeffers that appeared the same year as a book by Wallace Stevens, and those appearing the same year as one of Eliot's extremely kooky books.

Not only tameness, but sameness.

Sameness! It would follow somehow that someone is controlling the genetic breeding, and no new blood is coming in from the outside. So you have that sameness of the workshop. The workshops would be the breeding stations, I suppose.

I feel that the domestication is being done by two entities now: the universities, and the National Endowment for the Arts. When the government gives money, it results in domestication of the poet. I think that the National Endowment is an even worse catastrophe, in the long run, to the ecology of poetry than the universities. Talking yesterday to your class, I said, "Wayne understands the whole issue of the wildness that's involved with poetry, and how slowly animals in the wild learn to do things." You have grown slowly in poetry. So you're in a spot, actually, when you teach a workshop, because as you know, the funny thing about a workshop is that we want people to write fast, to write in their early twenties. That's impossible! They even want to get a job with it. How do you feel about that?

I agree entirely, and even though I make my living doing this, I always feel uncomfortable with a workshop situation because it seems to me to be such an essentially negative, or to borrow your metaphor, domesticating, function. Understandably, anyone working in a workshop situation, let's say on a continuing basis in a writing program, who feels as though he is learning to write, is going to feel that he is being taught to do something: that he's being taught how to write a poem. The things that will happen to him and to others he will see working in the workshop, are the things that will finally become in his mind the paradigm for how to make poems. And yet, my own perception is that, unless we're awfully careful, that doesn't teach you to write poems. Often it teaches you how not *to do certain things. It teaches you how* not *to make gross mistakes that are going to be unacceptable.*

Ah, yes! Go on, give me an example.

The image I have is that a person brings in a poem, and

it has some good stuff in it but also has a bunch of bad, which everyone with some sophistication perceives as bad. You know, maybe it ends wrong. So the teacher immediately hits that poet on the nose with a newspaper and says, "Not here! Outside!" and so teaches him not to pee on the rug in the house. After a while he learns not to do that. He learns how to write poems without those mistakes in them. But is that the same as learning to write poetry? What I worry about is not getting the positive aspects of poetry in there. As you put it, "The growing into a sense of what's inside."

The poet bringing in a shallow ending to a poem can be taught not to do that. What you're saying is that we have poets who learn in the workshops not to make disastrous mistakes. But then what?

Another metaphor I use sometimes is that real poems have navels; you can always find a navel in a poem.

What is the navel? Do you mean, for example, the connection between Maude Gonne and Yeats through which the poem somehow flows?

No, I don't think so. I'm thinking of the sense of human imperfection, of the profoundly real divisions and tensions in the psyche, of the individual depth of human experience. That is still, in itself, rather wild.

I can hear a typical workshop poet say to you: "What do you mean? I wrote a poem on my grandfather last year and I made it very clear he went through certain experiences cutting wood or farming that I haven't. Now my admission is tension and it is anguish, it is a navel." What do you say to that?

*I think that the poem that we're talking about at the mo-
ment is the poem that, finally, lacks content. I think the
only content of a poem is the positive or true emotional
life of the individual.*

Then he or she might say, "You're being insulting to
me. I am twenty-three years old. I have a true emotional
life. What right do you have to say that I don't have
one?"

Who can answer that? But I know talking to you that
I am not talking with a twenty-four year old. You have
been working in poetry for fifteen to twenty years, and
your poetry has grown slowly stronger and stronger.
You know how long it took you to arrive at the place
where you are. Don't you find a contradiction between
your experience and the expectation of the workshop
student, who expects that within two years, if he studies
with you, he will have a manuscript acceptable enough
to get an MFA, and possibly get published? How do you
deal with that contradiction?

*I deal with it by agreeing with you and saying I accept
it. I try to tell students about it. Anyone who comes
into a program thinking he's going to learn shortcuts is
doomed to failure. There is no such thing as a shortcut.
I think that one can learn certain skills, certain devices,
and maybe indeed speed up the process of learning
poetry somewhat. But there are no real shortcuts.*

But they're still winning. They're winning because
they're receiving the knowledge that you have received
in fifteen years of writing poetry, and you are giving it
to them and they are accepting it. Both of you have the
tacit understanding that out of it will come a manu-
script acceptable for an MFA, and possibly for a pub-

lished book. So actually, even though you are warning the students about it, they are still winning and taking what they want and you are giving it to them.

I certainly think that that is the case with many writing schools in this country.

I'm in the same situation. If I come into a college, even for one day, I can find no reason for not teaching what I know. But I'm still going along with the unreality of the student, who imagines that by listening to an older poet for a while, he or she will be able to substantially improve the manuscript, so it will be more likely to be published. This ignores everything that the Tao Te Ching talks about, in terms of the slow flow of human life, the slow growth of oak trees, and all of that. There's some kind of lie that the workshops, and visiting poets, are involved in. I'm involved in it.

Don't you think that the real problem lies somehow outside the expectations of the student? I think their expectation are *a problem, but perhaps there is a real problem also in the response of—I don't know what we're going to call it—the keepers of the system and the tradition, in their accepting and reinforcing that expectation.*

Who are the keepers of the system?

Well, I suppose book publishers and editors.

It is a responsibility of publishers not to publish so many books of poetry. But you know what's happened. With the National Endowment supporting presses, a young man or woman can start a press. The National Endowment does not pay him a salary, but he can use some of the money given him to pay at least for the secretarial work, which the wife or husband or friend may do in connection with a book. There's a lot of genial corruption going on in that area. Books get published without risk or sacrifice—that's a book that shouldn't be published. That may sound stupid. I hear people say that the more books of poetry published the better. I don't agree. First of all, one often notices that poets who publish a book early often end up repeating themselves later on. Readers want to be amused. If you do something well—and we all know poets who have done that early on—the readers constantly urge the poet to do the same thing over again. By thirty-five he hasn't grown a bit. If he hadn't published early, but waited till his thirties, then, like Wallace Stevens or Walt Whitman, both of whom didn't publish until their late thirties and early forties, more growth would have taken place before *and* after that time. It seems to me that workshops are extremely destructive in the way they prepare students for publishing ten years too early.

You would agree, then, that that system is a system of avoidance of pain? It seems to me that's the exact opposite way of going about discovering how to write profound poetry.

That's very interesting, because the best part of workshops, probably, is the pain that a writer feels when someone criticizes his poem in public. But it hadn't occurred to me that this may be a substitute for the long-range pain which a person working alone feels, when he feels despair looking at his manuscript, knowing it is inadequate.

I've had that experience so many times. I'd prepare a group of two dozen poems, in my twenties, type them up excitedly, and then discover I had only two or three poems. Then I would fall into a depression for several weeks. After a few months I would put together another group of twenty, and this time find again in despair that maybe five were genuine. This solitary pain, with no one to relieve it, is a typical situation of the wild animal writer. The workshops take away some of that pain by having someone there to encourage you. Your friends in the workshop encourage you; "This is better than your last poem. I'd publish it." And I guess that amounts to an avoidance of pain.

I found out recently that one of the stronger labors in my life has been the labor to avoid unpleasant emotions. Pain is probably one of those.

I worry too about the writer's perception of what a poem is. I worry that the person will come genuinely to believe, as he's working on and living with a poem, that doing certain things is equivalent to the poem itself and to the basic instinct or impulse to poetry. I worry about the possible insinuation of a kind of "imitation" as the essential gesture of poetry. What do you think?

Let's go back to the image of domestication. In the wild state males fight each other. One of the things that has disappeared in the last twenty years in poetry has been the conflict between the young man and the old one. And the progress of the generations does not move well in any field unless the younger scientists or poets are willing to attack the older ones. Ortega y Gasset describes the process clearly in *Meditations on Quixote*. He begins four or five generations before Galileo. Astronomers then loved their teachers. But the young astronomers worked hard to find the flaw in their teacher's work. Each generation by that labor overturned the one before. This constant thought movement finally led to the astounding achievements of Galileo. Ortega makes it clear that in a healthy situation that is how males behave.

I participated in that a little when I started *The Fifties.* I started the magazine precisely to attack Allen Tate's and Robert Penn Warren's view of poetry. The reason for that is not because I hated Allen Tate. As you remember, in the fifties the shade from Eliot and Pound and Tate and William Carlos Williams was a heavy shade. It was necessary to clear some ground, so there'd be a place for new pine trees to grow. That clearing is not being done now. Perhaps my generation is casting shade now. The younger poets are not attacking Galway enough, or Merwin, or Wright, or Creeley, or Ginsberg. They're a little slow in attacking me too. The women don't attack Levertov or Rich. The younger poets are being nice boys and girls. Partly it is cultural, the sixties' obsession with good feeling. But the normal process of human growth from generation to generation involves, as Ortega details, the new generation attacking the older one. And attacking them strongly, wiping them out as far as possible.

Just as Eliot did when he attacked Browning.

Oh yes; Eliot's work seems a new thing to us, invented, but Eliot's old man was Browning. And Eliot, by using allusions where Browning used a standard, straightforward continuity of detail, actually was attacking and overturning Browning's dramatic monologue, and it was felt at the time. All the Browning people thought *The Waste Land* was absolutely disgusting. *Time* magazine called it a hoax. Eliot was pointing out that Browning was boring in the way he strings his perceptions of human beings together with no empty place for our imagination to enter. So Eliot decided to do a different portrait—for example the portrait of his wife in *The Waste Land,* and he left big gaps in the portrait. In fact, he just left out entire arms and legs. *The Waste Land* is an attack on Browning and a victory over him. Eliot also did a lot of attacking in criticism; he was a very serious critic. This struggle is related to a fact about male animals Konrad Lorenz discovered. In the wild, two males, let's say pheasant cocks, spend some weeks in the spring settling the issue of territory. Perhaps a rooster will want a quarter of a mile. The defeated male retires from the territory. When the fights are over, the rooster who remains accepts the first female who enters the territory. Essentially he has cleared ground so that there will be enough for himself, the hen, and the chicks to eat. The stag fights are similar. A stag may need five or ten square miles, but the only way to insure enough space is for the males to fight. No one understood that before. People in the nineteenth century thought that stags were fighting over the females, but actually they're fighting over the space. My metaphor then is that the younger poets, in failing to attack Merwin, or Rich, or Levertov, or me, or Ginsberg, or Simpson, or Hall, or Ed Dorn, are not doing their job. They are not making a place for their chicks.

You mean, of course, they are not attacking them in criticism and reviews. But you mean in their work too? That they're not attacking them there also?

I think it's mainly the absence of public criticism that's a disaster: the disappearance of criticism. Private criticism doesn't count. We notice magazines with nothing but poems in them, not a single review or "idea" article. The cliché of the last ten years is, "I want to say something positive. If I can't say something positive I don't want to say anything at all." There is a fear of having and using power. Imagine a stag in the north woods saying, "Well, I want to like all the other stags. I don't want any power. So I'll just take my horns off." To me one of the disasters that's happened is that so many poets have gotten the habit of emphasizing their own work, and have been unwilling to face head-on the poetry of others, older or even their own age. Ashbery is an example, Berrigan, Wakowski, Dubie, Gluck, Ginsberg. Many poets at poetry readings read nothing but their own work.

The point is not that Eliot disliked Browning; he never met Browning. It was an attack of psychic energy only. But think of this situation by contrast: the medium generation of poets, Donald Justice, Marvin Bell, Dick Hugo, etc., are teaching in a college. The younger poets are grateful to poets like Justice and Bell for teaching them. This gratefulness to the older poet prevents them from doing the natural thing, which is to take the work seriously, turn on poets in the older generation, and attack them. Justice and Bell and Hugo don't want to be attacked, and they encourage the good feeling.

I was thinking of this only yesterday: that the university system, which seems in the beginning so sweet, where one can go in as a younger poet and find an older poet whom you admire to work with, causes everything to break down. We're living in a swamp of mediocrity, poetry of the Okefenokee, in which a hundred and fifty mediocre books—and they're mediocre partly because the men writing them are somehow not completely males, because they haven't broken through to their own psychic ground—are published every year. When a man or woman succeeds in grasping what his or her master has done, and breaking through it, he doesn't create something artificial. He enters through his belly button into the interior space inside himself. And there, to everyone's surprise, are new kinds of grass, and new kinds of trees, and all of that!

So that suddenly makes the term "tame" a real, living metaphor.

And it explains why, though it was so good in a way to get rid of the New Criticism—New Criticism by the way was itself a tiger, and John Crowe Ransom was Captain Carpenter. They attacked the life work of the historical critics with ferocity, and evicted it from the English departments. Then the *Kenyon Review* started to get a little pesty, but no one killed it, it just died. Maybe English departments believe in eternity. The result, I find, is a tameness and smugness in many younger male poets, the young female poets are tame also, and there is a tameness in criticism. Oftentimes I'll open a poetry magazine and there will be seventy pages of poetry and not one article. I hear poets who are proud never to have written criticism. They warble: "I'm very sensitive, you know. I'm a special person. Criticism should be done by corrupt types like university professors and journalists. I just love poetry."

There's one stupid magazine out in California. Do you remember that one *Poetry* . . .? It's published in a format like *APR*.

Oh yes. Poetry Now.

Yes! A really stupid one! This magazine says, "I'm going to publish a review now of a book." And the book review consists of the title of the book, the name of the author, and one or two of the poems. And *APR* doesn't really have much criticism. It's edited by committee, and they specialize in thirty-page articles on Ashbery that no one can finish.

That's absolutely true, and that's a complaint that has been voiced by a lot of serious poets and critics lately. Donald Hall wrote recently about the need for real criticism. And Marvin Bell also once said, commenting on some negative criticism I had written of a book, that it was really important for us to keep writing criticism, and to keep reviewing. I was glad to hear Marvin say that.

I think it's a good idea for each poet to take a vow to review, let's say, two books every six months. It's a part of his discipline. And he doesn't wait to be assigned a review. He writes it and then finds a place for it later.

When my own generation began to write, around 1954-58 or so, poetry and the persona were considered linked, and both were considered a child of the iambic rhythm. Allen Ginsberg, following Whitman, attacked those linkages by talking about his own life in *Howl*. And Jim Wright altered the relation of the iambic line to English poetry by bringing in whole areas of things that Keats had never thought about in relation to grief among the coal miners. And when he brought the slag heaps in, he found, following Trakl, that some new kind of consciousness in the twentieth century passes to the reader through the precise image, conscious and unconscious. Ginsberg uses mainly the mental or general image. I studied the precise image a great deal too. But we must see that the image is not a final solution. Many young poets are still writing calmly, almost smugly, in the image, without looking around. Obsession with image can become a psychic habit as much as obsession with persona, and we need new ways of bringing forward consciousness. Some hints have appeared, but few younger poets have cleared ground for themselves in that area. They have simply accepted the whole discovery of the image as it comes through, through Neruda, through Trakl, and the Americans.

And you could also say that this shows that the American male is solving his father problem less and less. It's quite possible that a hundred years ago there was much more resentment of the son against the father. The father after all controlled the keys to the economy, particularly if he were a master and you were the apprentice. Now the son can avoid living the whole father problem by going into a completely different field, say, computers. Maybe he doesn't realize that he still has to confront the father in some way. I think this failure in the artistic world is a reflection of a desire of the young males to live in a state of comfort, as opposed to the terrific state of tension and anger with your father which was more the situation a few generations ago.

Speaking of criticism, it seems to me that one sees a resurgence, or upsurge, or something like that, in the last few years, of what I would call the "new neoclassicism."

All right, give me an example.

I'm thinking of the criticism written by Harold Bloom, and poetry by people such as Ammons and Ashbery.

And in what sense is that neoclassical?

Well, I think the way in which it emphasizes strictly formal and intellectual concerns and almost wholly denies the emotional.

Ashbery would say that his poetry is actually rather sur-realisitic. So how can you reconcile those two adjectives?

Ashbery is surrealistic at times, that's true. But I find very little emotion. I find that his surrealism much of the time is not getting at other, more disturbing realities, but keeping away from them.

I follow what you're saying, because if you examine something like *Beowulf,* it's perfectly clear that neither the poet nor the reader can go on eighty lines without going into a powerful gut feeling like deep thankfulness, or anger. One can go through pages of Ashbery and never find any emotions beyond those that the cerebellum is capable of. Neoclassical critics are writing again, suggest-ing that perhaps Yvor Winters was right, after all. Robert Pinsky is one.

And I'm thinking of Pinsky too.

Are you? The old dualistic line doesn't change, it seems, no matter what else changes. The Yvor Winters types just remain. They are like the old VW Beetle and remain the same from generation to generation. But the acad-emies have also produced a new sort of academic critic, and Bloom surely belongs to them.

An odd thing about Bloom's criticism is that it consists of "forwarding" a poet.

That's interesting. It hasn't always been that way. Samuel Johnson was a critic who was willing to tackle even Shakespear. He'll say this scene with Cordelia is absolutely absurd, or he'll declare about a certain pas-sage, "I'm sorry to say that human beings do not speak this way." In most cases he's right. A critic's task is to find where genuine feeling is not touching the words, or not nourishing the words, and so point out the fake areas so that others become aware of the problem. Mencken did that, constantly, with every speech a president gave. Edmund Wilson did it with novels. You can't appreciate the great unless you see where it fails. But Harold Bloom decides to "creatively" uplift his subjects, so instead of criticizing what is there in the shadowy area, being uncomfortable, he elevates Ashbery and Ammons, a very unusual thing for a critic to do. What he is elevating upward is some kind of a . . . , well, I suppose to go back to your image, it's poets that know precisely how not to pee on the rug. They never do that; they're very well mannered. They ostensibly have a shirttail relation to Wallace Stevens. But they do not have the grandeur of Stevens. Ashbery has become an utterly academic poet. Academic poetry in the fifties was recognizable by emotional anemia and English meter. Now it is recognizable by fake French surrealism and emotional anemia. In Ashbery there is no anger, there is no world. There are no trees, there are no animals, there are no women; there is no oppression, there are no dictators; there's actually no intense compassion! There are no characters as in Chaucer. You have an academic anemia disguised as the French avant garde and almost none of the critics, young or old, have the guts to see through it. Ashbery has a kind of genius. But I also feel that his poetry is empty and academic.

What about the use of the unconscious in American poetry today? For a time, after the work you and others did in the fifties and sixties, breaking down a parochialism of the imagination, it seemed that a good many poets were beginning to respond to this in their work. But now

I see poems in which the signs ought to be pointing in that direction, but there is no road into the power of the unconscious where the wild is, to go back and borrow your metaphor. Is this an example of what you were just saying about Ashbery, finding dodges to make it seem that one is doing one thing when in fact one isn't?

That's very interesting. D. H. Lawrence wrote of this progression, using the image of the umbrella. Kafka or Conrad, let's say, rips holes in the umbrella; then one sees through to the night sky and the stars, which in this case represent the unconscious. That's rather scary. Poe did that. What happens next? A Longfellow type appears; he makes another umbrella and this time paints stars on the inside of it. And grateful readers say, "Look at that sky! Look at the wonderful stars up there!" Andy Warhol does that in relation to what Max Ernst was doing. It may be that this sort of thing goes in waves. After all, some nonliterary Conrad in the psyche tore off the umbrella and showed Americans the Vietnam war. So the whole nation insists on comfortable stuff again. "Don't scare me." Writers who want to deal with the true unconscious will be alone for a while.

Do you think there is a kind of correspondence between the fact of, on the one hand, the presence of this domestication of the poet learning forms and formulae, and on the other hand this academicism? Because academicism doesn't want the wildness anyway?

I went to the Iowa workshop a year. In general what was being taught was technique. That was because there had been with the New Critics a swing away from Whitman and William Carlos Williams back to using English models again. If you look at *New Poets of England and America,* published in 1958, you see most models are English. But during the sixties most workshops, graduate at least, stopped teaching iambic technique. Why don't the workshops then emphasize the deep content, the angers, the confrontations, that you find in Neruda or Yeats; the political content that you find in Brecht, and so on? Why aren't those being emphasized? Well, as you so wonderfully say with the image of the rolled newspaper, some form of behavioral training takes place instead. Students are taught to write, as David Ignatow says sarcastically, "the perfect poem."

We have never before faced what it's like in the culture when hundreds of people want to write poetry and want to be instructed in it. In the Middle Ages, in the Renaissance, there weren't that many people who wanted to be painters; but if they did they went to a studio and entered into a deep father-son relationship with a painter, privately, one-to-one in his workshop. Now we are trying to instruct hundreds of beginning poets in the universities. We don't know how to instruct in that area. We know how to instruct a hundred engineers, or a thousand computer technicians, but that knowledge doesn't help. If you read a history of Ch'an Buddhism, you'll notice that Buddhism faced the same problem. It began with just a few people, and later huge numbers of people wanted Buddhist instruction. Ch'an Buddhism does not involve doctrine; it involves the same kind of thing we're talking about, breaking through the ego and getting down to the unconscious, breaking through conventional attitudes and getting down to the real ones, breaking through your society face and getting down to your genuine face.

They learned how to do that. Their method doesn't resemble a workshop. They didn't teach politeness or the smooth surface. They didn't teach "the poetry of fans" as Neruda would say. The teacher wouldn't assign an exercise to be done at the desk for the following week, but his plan would involve something entirely outside the building. Perhaps a man might come in and say, "I want to learn something about Buddhism. I want to get my degree in Buddhism in a year and a half. What books shall I read? You want me to do meditation exercises now?" The monk would say, "No, I don't think so. You go out in the woods there, and build yourself a little house, and live there six months, and then come back and see me."

"What shall I do?"

"Oh, that's your business. I don't know; you do what you want to. Don't have any servants or anything like that. Get your own water and bake your own bread."

So the man is out there for six months all by himself, and he is in charge of his own body. Finally he comes back and says, "OK, I've done it. I've built my house and I'm ready now. Will you give me instruction?"

"Oh no, I don't think so. Actually we need a meditation hut out there very bad. I think you had better build that."

"What do I build it out of?"

"Oh, stones. There're a lot stones on that hill there. You can use those stones and build a house up there."

"How long will it take me?"

"Oh, six or eight months. When you're done come see me."

He comes back and says, "Well, OK. I'm done now. I want my instruction in meditation."

"Well, you haven't been moving around very much. Probably a good thing you see a little land. Why don't you take a trip around China? Make about a six-month trip. I'm busy. You come back, see me in six months."

And if he's willing to go through all that—actually

during all that he is *doing* something and getting away from his mental attitude—he has received instruction. The instruction throws him back on his own body. By making him do things he understands that art is not a matter of getting something from a teacher. Art is a matter of going into your own resources and building. You may even have shown the student that it's necessary to build a house out of stone.

We're doing the opposite. We allow people to come to a workshop and receive immediately what you, for example, have worked ten to fifteen years to learn yourself. A nineteen-year-old student comes to your office, and because our teaching is structured so, we offer him that material right away. We can't say that plan is wrong or right. We can only say the Buddhists learned not to teach that way.

I must say that if I were going to teach a workshop on a long-range basis I would try to introduce some method of that sort. I would refuse to meet with the students regularly; but they would have to live away from the campus, in the woods or desert. They wouldn't be able to get any instruction until they had earned it, by breaking dependencies, doing things for themselves. One might say to a student, "After you have your hut, translate twenty-five poems from a Rumanian poet."

"But I don't know Rumanian."

"Well then, that's your first job. You learn Rumanian, translate the twenty-five poems, and then come back to see me, and I'll tell you what I think about 'the deep image.'"

One learns a lot by translating a great poet. By that method, we get closer to the actual way that art was taught in the Renaissance. You might go to Rubens, for example, and say: "I would like to be your student. Would you teach me your philosophy of painting?" And he might say, "Well, there's a shoe missing down in the left hand corner. Please paint it so it looks exactly like the other shoe. Don't talk, paint."

What do you suppose accounts for the almost total absence of this sort of attitude from the writers in our society?

This contrast between "doing," which is the ancient way of learning, and "studying," which we want to do, I think is connected to the difference between the working class, who are always doing, and the white-collar classes.

In the Midwest, most of our grandparents or great-grandparents came here as immigrants, if from Scandinavia, they belonged to the working classes. Virtually all Norwegians were working class in the nineteenth century. So most of the immigrants were working class. But, the next generation doesn't want to be that way; they want to go to college. They want to rise.

The phenomenon of the university-based poet I think is linked to this longing. Many grandsons and granddaughters of immigrants are proud to be MFA's because it proves that they're not working class.

You know, Gary Snyder said something not unrelated to that in an interview we recently published. The interviewer could hardly believe what he was hearing when Snyder said that if a person wanted to learn how to be a poet he ought to go find a person who could "do" something well, and learn how to do it with him. Find, for example, a good carpenter. Or find a good mechanic, and then just stick with him for a while! Live with him, hang around him. Watch him and help him work. Learn to do it, maybe for two or three years.

The interviewer finally said to him, "Are we still talking about poetry?" And Snyder said, "Fuckin' A we're still talking about poetry. You learn how to write poetry by learning how to do anything really well and proper."

Beautiful!

So that's surely related to the kind of thing you're talking about.

Surely it's related to Thoreau's care in building his house in which he learned how to put together a chapter.

In Worcester, Massachusetts, community poetry readings have been going for eight or nine years now. They have a wonderfully serious duo there: Mike True and Franny Quinn. They began the reading in the downtown library, which isn't a university setting. The community comes. Young poets now are glad to come and read at the library. Meanwhile Franny has been setting up readings in four or five places on the outskirts of Worcester, city halls or senior citizens' places or bars.

A poet says, "You know, I've been around a lot; I'd like to read at the library." And Franny says, "We'd like that, but we 'd like you to read at three of these places also." Well, you drive out to an old town hall at six o'clock on Friday evening, and there're four old men sitting there, and they've never heard a serious poem spoken in their life. So it's not a thrilling reading. There's no standing ovation. However, if you want to read at the library you do that too. So the poet says, "OK." And the old men like to have young men come out and tell them about their marriages.

Then Mike or Franny might say, "That was fine. Now I'd like you to set up the program for the next group of poets we have coming through."

"What does that involve?"

"Well, it would mean going to, say, Lowell, and starting from scratch there to set up the reading places and dates."

"I can't..., ah, I'm not gonna..., I can't organ-.... ah, I'm not organizing...that's not..."

"Why not?"

"Well, I'm a poet."

"What does that mean?"

"Well, I'm just not an organizer. Some people do that well, really, but I just write poetry."

Then Franny might say, "I have one bit of news. I'm a poet and I've been organizing for eight and a half years, and you've just received the benefit of the organization. The job here would be to talk to the city council. Convince them the idea would work, ask for a spot, etc., and do some work on the posters."

There's a great resistence to this, because being a poet with an MFA is a status symbol. Or even being "a poet" implies that in this country. So the resistance to crafting and learning by doing may go back to a fear of being working class.

*   *   *   *   *

What is the effect on poets of all the "sameness" you spoke of earlier?

Perhaps poetry is developing a protective camouflage of brown and gray feathers. A poetry shelf has fewer and fewer peacocks with long tails, like Robinson Jeffers. Probably this heavy breeding is nice. And it's possible that hawks don't see some gray birds and don't attack them, you know.

But if a person just beginning to read poetry walks into a bookstore and starts paging through all the boring gray and brown books of poetry, what does that do for the readership of poetry? When too much boring poetry is published, poets themselves begin to lose morale. I'm wondering how that could change.

I assume that the number of workshops will continue to increase. Then as the job offers go down, the new poets' will becomes more and more tame, and more and more like the last generation. Suppose a number of poets would like a new position at Wisconsin, but Wisconsin wants to hire Galway Kinnell. That means that unconsciously, even consciously, the young poets will try to be more like Galway Kinnell. William Carlos Williams did not want to be like Galway Kinnell. Cummings or Marianne Moore did not have bureaucracy mentality. Each wanted to be wild separately! I don't see any possibility but it's getting worse.

It may also be that poets will be afraid to risk doing the really different thing, that might seem to be profoundly true to them nonetheless, for fear of being accused of peeing on the floor.

Oh, indeed! That's right! I'm sure that the reviewers of Pound's early work, which had a lot of freaky originality, accused him constantly of being poorly housetrained. What would originality look like today? Perhaps it would involve intimate revelations not confessional, such as Akhmatova writes.

I don't believe originality will increase if the poetry becomes more primitive. Jerry Rothenberg to the contrary, most primitive poetry is probably boring. After you've said, "Here comes the otter, here comes the otter, here comes the otter. A woka-woka-woka! The bird flew down from the sky. Dawn is coming, Wok-i-way, I'm alive." You say that about ninety-eight times. . . . We live in an industrial society. I love the oral quality of primitive poetry, but how can a university be oral?

The problem is, how does poetry maintain itself as a vivid, highly colored, living thing? It's possible that originality comes when the man or woman disobeys the collective. The cause of tameness is fear. The collective says: "If you do your training well and become a nice boy or girl, we will love you." We want that. So a terrible fear comes. It is a fear that we will lose the love of the collective. I have felt it intensely. What the collective offers is not even love, that is what is so horrible, but a kind of absence of loneliness. Its companionship is ambiguous, like mother love.

a vivid, highly colored

living thing

Ann Arbor   **The University of Michigan Press**